Alfred Gudeman

Syllabus on the History of classical Philology

Alfred Gudeman

Syllabus on the History of classical Philology

ISBN/EAN: 9783337230197

Printed in Europe, USA, Canada, Australia, Japan

Cover: Foto ©ninafisch / pixelio.de

More available books at **www.hansebooks.com**

SYLLABUS

ON THE

HISTORY OF CLASSICAL PHILOLOGY

BY

DR. ALFRED GUDEMAN

JOHNS HOPKINS UNIVERSITY

Genera gustamus non bibliothecas excutimus.—QUINTILIAN

BOSTON, U. S. A.

PUBLISHED BY GINN & COMPANY

1892

PREFATORY NOTE.

This Syllabus was originally prepared for a course of lectures on the history of classical philology, given at the Johns Hopkins University; it is now published with the hope that, in the absence of a compendious manual such as I have in preparation, it may prove helpful to a wider circle of classical students.

JUNE 1, 1892.   A. G.

CONTENTS.

SYLLABUS ON THE HISTORY OF CLASSICAL PHILOLOGY.

A. General Introduction.

I. a. Φιλόλογος—its original meaning and semasiological development.

First met with in *Plato (e. g.* Theaet., p. 146 *a*; Laches, p. 188; Rep., p. 582; Leges, p. 641 *e*). Opp. to μισόλογος, βραχύλογος. Equivalent to πολύλογος, φιλόσοφος. φιλολογία = παιδεία (μουσική). Cf. Plato, Phaed. 61 *a*; Isoc. de Antid. 296: εὐτραπελίαν καὶ φιλολογίαν οὐ μικρὸν ἡγοῦνται συμβαλέσθαι μέρος, πρὸς τὴν τῶν λόγων παιδείαν, etc. *Alexandrian Period:* Equivalent to φιλομαθής, πολυΐστωρ (cf. Plut. Alex., c. 8). In this sense first applied to *Eratosthenes*, and among the Romans to *Ateius Capito.* Cf. Sueton. de gram., p. 108 R. "Philologi appellationem assumpsisse videtur quia, sicut Eratosthenes qui primus hoc cognomen sibi vindicavit, multiplici variaque doctrina censebatur." *Roman Period:* φιλολογεῖν = learned conversation. Cf. Cic. ad fam. XVI 21; Plut. Cato Min. 6; Ps. Plut. Vit. X Orat., p. 844 D. φιλόλογοι opp. to πολιτικοί—Plut. Lyc. 42. Opp. to φιλόσοφος—Vita Plotini, p. 116: φιλόλογος μὲν ὁ Λυγγῖνος, φιλόσοφος δὲ μηδαμῶς. Opp. to ἀπαίδευτος—Stob. Floril. 428, 53. Philologus = vir studiosus, doctus—Cic. ad Att. XIII 12, 3; Plut. de aud. poet. 30 *d*. More closely allied to philologist in the modern sense in *Seneca*, Ep. 108, 29, quoted below.

b. Γραμματικός (γραμματική, sc. τέχνη)—its original meaning and semasiological development.

Conversant with γράμματα (Plato, Phil. 17; Crat., p. 341; Arist. Pol. VIII 3; Categ. 9). γραμματιστής = a teacher of γράμματα (Plato, Prot. 312; Legg. VII 812). *Alexandrian Period: Clem. Alex.* Στρωμ. I, p. 309: Ἀπολλόδωρος (Ἀντόδωρος?) ὁ Κυμαῖος (unknown) πρῶτος τοῦ κριτικοῦ εἰσηγήσατο τοὔνομα καὶ γραμματικὸς προσηγορεύθη. Ἔνιοι δὲ Ἐρατοσθένη

τὸν Κυρηναῖον φασὶν ἐπειδὴ ἐξέδωκεν οὗτος βιβλία δύο γραμματικὰ ἐπί-
γραψας. ὠνομάσθη δὲ γραμματικός, ὡς νῦν (3d. cent.) ὀνομάζομεν,
πρῶτος Πραξιφάνης (c. 300 B. C.). Γραμματική acc. to *Dionysius*
Thrax : Ἐμπειρία ὡς ἐσὶ τὸ πλεῖστον τῶν παρὰ ποιηταῖς τε κὰι συγγρα-
φεῦσι λεγομένων. *Six* subdivisions :

1. Ἀνάγνωσις ἐντριβὴς κατὰ προσῳδίαν
2. Ἐξήγησις κατὰ ποιητικοὺς τρόπους
3. Γλωσσῶν καὶ ἱστοριῶν πρόχειρος ἀπόδοσις
4. Ἐτυμολογίας εὕρεσις
5. Ἀναλογίας ἐκλογισμός
$\left.\right\}$ = τέχνη μικρά, ἀτελεστέρα.

6. Κρίσις ποιημάτων—ὃ δὴ κάλλιστόν ἐστι $\left.\right\}$ = τ. μακρά, ἐντελής.
πάντων ἐν τῇ τέχνῃ

Sext. Emp. adv. Gramm. I 4 (according to Apollonios Dyscolos?) Γραμματική: 1. τεχνικόν; 2. ἱστορικόν; 3. ἰδιαίτε-
ρον. a. ἐξηγητικόν; b. κριτικόν; c. διορθωτικόν.
Roman Period: Sueton. de gramm., p. 103 Rf.: "Appellatio
grammaticorum Graeca consuetudine invaluit sed initio *litte-
rati* vocabantur. Cornelius quoque Nepos libello quo dis-
tinguit litteratum ab erudito, litteratos vulgo quidem appellari
ait eos qui diligenter aliquid et acute scienterque possint aut
dicere aut scribere, ceterum proprie sic appellandos poetarum
interpretes qui a Graecis grammatici nominentur." *Cic. de
orat.* I 42, 187: grammatica = poetarum pertractio, histori-
arum cognitio, verborum interpretatio, pronuntiandi quidem
sonus ; cp. also Orat. I 22; de div. I 11 ; *Quint.* I 4, II 1, 4
(grammatica = litteratura), and *Sen.* Ep. 88.

c. Κριτικός.
   Among *the Greeks:* First found in *Ps. Plat. Axioch.* 366 E :
ὁπόταν δὲ εἰς τὴν ἑπταετίαν ἀφίκηται πολλοὺς πόνους διαντλῆσαν, παιδα-
γωγοὶ καὶ γραμματισταὶ καὶ παιδοτρίβαι τυραννοῦντες. αὐξομένου δὲ
κριτικοί, γεωμέτραι, τακτικοί, πολὺ πλῆθος δεσποτῶν. Κριτικός as
a synonym of γραμματικός. Γραμματική sometimes made
subordinate to κριτική. Cf. *Schol. ad Dionys. Thr.*, p. 673,
19 : ἐπιγέγραπται γὰρ τὸ παρὸν σύγγραμμα κατὰ μέν τινας περὶ γραμματικῆς, κατὰ δὲ ἑτέρους περὶ κριτικῆς τέχνης. κριτικὴ δὲ λέγεται ἡ τέχνη
ἐκ τοῦ καλλίστου μέρους. *Bekker, Anecd. Gr.*, p. 1140 : τὸ πρότερον κριτικὴ ἐλέγετο (sc. ἡ γραμματική) καὶ οἱ ταύτην μετίοντες κριτικοί.
Dio Chrys. 53 : οὐ μόνον Ἀρίσταρχος καὶ Κράτης καὶ ἕτεροι πλείους
τῶν ὕστερον γραμματικῶν κληθέντων, πρότερον δὲ κριτικῶν. *Sext.
Emp.* adv. *Gramm.*, §248 : Ταυρίσκος γοῦν ὁ Κράτητος ἀκουστὴς
ὥσπερ οἱ ἄλλοι κριτικοί, ὑποτάσσων τῇ κριτικῇ τὴν γραμματικήν, etc.

Among the Romans: *Cic. ad fam.* IX 10, 1 (quoted by Suet., p. 111): profert alter, opinor, duobus versiculis expensum Niciae; alter Aristarchus hos ὀβελίζει. Ego tamquam *criticus* antiquus iudicaturus sum, utrum sint τοῦ ποιητοῦ an παρεμβεβλημένοι. *Hor. Ep.* II 1, 51 : ut *critici* dicunt. Apparently not found elsewhere in Latin, grammaticus being the word commonly used. For the distinction between the various termini, the locus classicus is found in *Senec. Ep.* 108, 29 : Cum Ciceronis librum de republica prendit hinc *philologus* aliquis, hinc *grammaticus*, hinc *philosophiae* deditus alius alio curam suam mittit. *Philosophus* admiratur contra iustitiam dici tam multa potuisse. Cum ad hanc eandem lectionem *philologus* accessit, hoc subnotat : duos Romanos reges esse, quorum alter patrem non habet, alter patrem : nam de Servii matre dubitatur. Anci pater nullus, Numae nepos dicitur. Praeterea notat eum, quem nos dictatorem dicimus et in historiis ita nominari legimus, apud antiquos magistrum populi vocatum. Hodieque id exstat in auguralibus libris et testimonium est quod qui ab illo nominetur, magister equitum est. Aeque notat Romulum perisse solis defectione, provocationem ad populum etiam a regibus fuisse ; id ita in pontificalibus libris et alii putant et Fenestella. Eosdem libros cum *grammaticus* explicuit primum verba expressa, reapse dici a Cicerone id est re ipsa, in commentarium refert nec minus sepse id est se ipse, deinde transit ad ea quae consuetudo saeculi mutavit tamquam ait Cicero . . 'ab ipsa calce . . revocati' hanc quam nunc in circo cretam vocamus, calcem antiqui dicebant. Deinde Ennianos colligit versus et in primis illos de Africano scriptos . . . Felicem deinde se putat quod invenerit unde visum sit Vergilio dicere, 'quem super ingens porta tonat caeli'—Ennium, hoc ait, Homero subripuisse, Ennio Vergilium, esse enim apud Ciceronem in his ipsis de republica libris hoc epigramma Enni. Modern literature on this subject :

I. Classen, De grammaticae Graecae primordiis; Bonn, 1829. *Lobeck,* Phrynichus, p. 392 ff. *K. Lehrs,* De vocabulis φιλόλογος, γραμματικός, κριτικός (Appendix to Herodiani Scripta Tria, Berlin, 1857). *Gräfenhan,* Gesch. der class. Philologie, I 336 ff.; III 4 ff. *Steinthal,* Gesch. d. Sprachwissenschaft bei den Griech. u. Röm. II², p. 14 ff. *Susemihl,* Gesch. der Alexand. Literat. I, p. 327 (see below).

II. PHILOLOGY IN MODERN TIMES:

Its various definitions, subdivisions and its scope.

In a *narrower* sense—Grammar, Lexicology, Textual Criticism, Hermeneutics, aesthetic or literary criticism ('Higher Criticism').

In a *wider* sense, it includes the study of ancient life in all its various, political, social and intellectual phases, as handed down to us in the literary, epigraphic and monumental documents of Greece and Rome.

Fr. Ast, Grundriss der Phil. 1808. *A. Böckh*, Encyclopaedie und Methodologie, etc., ed. by Klussmann; Leipzig, 1886. *Fr. Ritschl*, Opusc. V 1 ff. *Fr. Haase*, Ersch u. Gruber, III, sec. 23, pp. 374–422. *H. Reichardt*, Die Gliederung der Philologie; Tübingen, 1846. *E. Hübner*, Encyclop., p. 3 ff.

III. METHODS OF TREATMENT.

1. The SYNCHRONISTIC or ANNALISTIC METHOD.
   a. History of a *single period*. *E. g.* the Alexandrian, the Renaissance.
   b. Philological history of a *single author*. *E. g.* Homeric criticism; Aristotle, history of his works (Shute).
   c. History of an *individual scholar* and his influence (Biography and Bibliography). *E. g. Monk*, Life of Bentley; *O. Ribbeck*, Ritschl, 'Ein Beitrag zur Gesch. der class. Philologie'; *D. Ruhnken*, Elogium Hemsterhusii; *Wyttenbach*, Elogium Ruhnkenii; *M. Pattison*, Casaubon.

2. The EIDOGRAPHIC METHOD.
   a. e. g. The science of Greek Grammar (Bernhardy, Steinthal).
   b. e. g. The history of Hermeneutics and Textual Criticism (Blass), Epigraphy (G. Hinrichs, E. Hübner, Th. Mommsen).

3. The ETHNOGRAPHIC or GEOGRAPHIC METHOD.
   a. *History of a particular school, e. g.* at Alexandria or in Pergamum (Parthey, Wegener).
   b. *Philological history of a single nation, e. g.* the Germans (Bursian), the Dutch (L. Müller).

B. History of Classical Philology.

General bibliography: *I. A. Fabricius*, Bibliotheca Graeca, ed. Harles; 12 voll., 1809. *Id.*, Bibliotheca Latina, ed. Ernesti; 2 voll., 1774. *E. Hübner*, Bibliographie der classischen Alterthumswissenschaft; Berlin, 1889². *Urlichs*, in I. Müller's Handbuch, I 1, pp. 126.

I. THE GREEK PERIOD (5 cent.–146 B. C.).

Bibliography: *Gräfenhan*, Gesch. der class. Philologie, 4 voll.; Bonn, 1843–50. *Lersch*, Sprachphilosophie der Alten, 3 voll., 1841. *Steinthal*, Geschichte der Sprachwissenschaft bei den Griechen u. Römern, 2 vols.; Berlin, 1891². *E. Egger*, Essai sur l'Histoire de la Critique chez les Grecs; Paris, 1886², pp. 570.

1. THE PRE-ALEXANDRIAN PERIOD, 5 cent.–322 († Aristotle).

a. *The alleged recension of Homer by Peisistratus.*

Cf. *Wilamowitz*, Homer. Untersuch., p. 235 ff. *Flach*, Peisistratus u. seine literarische Thätigkeit; Tübingen, 1885. Also *Ritschl*, Opusc. I, pp. 31–60, 123 ff., 160–67, 196 ff.

b. The *Sophists*.

Cf. *W. O. Friedel*, De sophistarum studiis Homericis, Diss. Hallens. I, 1873, p. 127 ff. *Gräfenhan*, I, pp. 124–41. *L. Spengel*, Συναγωγὴ τεχνῶν, 1828. *Westermann*, Griech. Beredsamkeit, 1832. *Blass*, Griech. Beredsamkeit, Vol. I. *Cope*, Aristotle's Rhetoric, Vol. I, Introduction.

α. *Gorgias* of Leontini (arrived at Athens 427 B. C.).

Περὶ ὀνομάτων συνθέσεως—ἰσόκωλα πάρισα ὁμοιοτέλευτα. Oral instruction. A treatise on rhetoric falsely attributed to him by Dionysius, Diogenes Laertius and Quintilian. Cf. the literature cited above.

β. *Protagoras* of Abdera († 411 B. C.).

Περὶ ὀρθοέπειας—P. the first to distinguish grammatical moods and genders. Cp. Aristoph. Clouds, vv. 659 ff.

Cf. Classen, l. c., p. 28; Lersch, l. c., p. 18 ff.; Spengel, p. 52 ff., and the citations given above.

γ. *Prodicus* of Ceos (older contemporary of Socrates). Founder of synonymics.

Cf. Spengel, l. c., p. 46 ff.; Lersch, p. 15 ff.; *Welcker*, Rh. Mus. I, pp. 1–39, 563–643 (= Kl. Schr. II, pp. 393–541).

c. *Literary Criticism in Attic Comedy.*

Cp. Egger, l. c., pp. 37–89.

d. Plato (427–347) as a philologist.

(1) Grammar (ὄνομα, ῥῆμα).

(2) Etymology (esp. in the Cratylus).

(3) Exegesis (Poem of Simonides in the Protagoras).

(4) Aesthetic or Literary Criticism (esp. in the *Republic*).

Cf. Steinthal, I², pp. 41–152 (on the Cratylus).

e. The official copy of the three dramatists.

Cf. O. Korn, De publico Aesch., Soph., Eurip., fabularum exemplari Lycurgo auctore confecto, Bonn, 1863; Wilamowitz, Hermes, XIV 151; Eurip. Heracl. I, p. 130.

e. Aristotle of Stagira, 384–322.

Dio Chrysost. LIII, p. 553: Ἀριστοτέλης, ἀφ' οὗ φασι τὴν κριτικήν τε καὶ γραμματικὴν ἀρχὴν λαβεῖν.

(1) Edition of *Homer* (ἡ ἀπὸ τοῦ νάρθηκος; cf. Plut. Alex. 8: Strabo, XIII 594; Schol. Iliad. 21, 252; Schol. Theocr. I 34—Προβλήματα (?).

(2) Grammar, style, *rhetoric* (Poet. c. 24 ff.; Rhet., bk. III).

(3) *Aesthetic* criticism (Poetics, Περὶ ποιητῶν).

(4) Διδασκαλίαι, C. I. G. I 349 sqq.; C. I. A. I 971–77.

Ranke, Vita Aristophanis (in Thiersch, Plutus, 1830), p. 83 ff.; Richter, Arist. Wasps, Introd.; U. Köhler, Mittheil. d. Athen. Instit. III (1878), p. 112 f., 129 ff.

f. The Peripatetic School.

α. *Heracleides Ponticus*, pupil of Plato and Aristotle.

Cf. Gräfenhan, II, p. 63; *Unger*, Rh. Mus. 38, p. 461 ff.; *L. Cohn*, Comment. Reiffersch., Breslau, 1884.

β. *Theophrastus* of Eresos, 372–287/6.

(1) Περὶ κωμῳδίας (Athen. 261 *d*).

(2) Περὶ λέξεως (Dionys. Hal. de Lys. c. 14).

Cf. *H. Usener*, De Dionysii Hal. imitatione reliquiae, Bonn, 1889.

(3) Περὶ μέτρων, περὶ σολοικισμῶν, probably parts of (2). Cf. the catalogue of his writings given by Diog. Laert. (from Hermippos) V 42–50.

γ. *Aristoxenus* ὁ μουσικός, *of Tarentum*.

Περὶ τραγῳδοποιῶν (esp. on Soph.), περὶ τραγικῆς ὀρχήσεως, Σύμμικτα ὑπομνήματα περὶ μουσικῆς, περὶ μελοποιίας—Βίοι (philosophers and tragedians). Cf. *W. L. Mahne*, Diatribe de A., 1793, pp. 220.

δ. *Dicaearchus*, 347–287.

Ὑποθέσεις τῶν Εὐριπίδου καὶ Σοφοκλέους μύθων (hypothesis to Eur. Medea still extant).

Περὶ μουσικῶν ἀγώνων (Schol. Arist. Ran. 1335; Vesp. 1290). Cf. F. Osann, Beitr. zur griech. u. röm. Litteraturgesch. II, 1839, p 1 ff.; Pauly, R. E. II 996 ff.

g. *Praxiphanes of Rhodes* or Mytilene, floruit c. 300.

'Πρῶτος γραμματικός'; vid. Clem. Alex. cited above. Teacher of Aratus and Callimachus.

Works : Περὶ ποιητῶν, περὶ ἱστορίας, περὶ ποιημάτων.

L. Preller, De Praxiphane (Ausgewählte Aufsätze, Berlin, 1864); Suse- mihl, I, p. 144 ff.; Wilamowitz, Hermes, XII, p. 326 ff.; R. Hirzel, Hermes, XIII, p. 46 ff.

h. *Antigonos of Carystos*, born c. 295.

(1) Lives of *contemporary philosophers*.

(2) Lives of *Greek sculptors and painters*.

Cf. *Wilamowitz*, Antigonos von Carystos (Philol. Unters. IV, pp. 356) ; *Susemihl*, I, pp. 468–75, 519–23; II 675.

2. The Alexandrian Period, 322 (or 305)–143 († Aristar- chus).

Chief work: *F. Susemihl*, Gesch. d. griech. Literat. in der Alexand. Zeit, 2 vols., 1892, pp. 907, 771.

General characteristics of the period. The great Library and Museum. Cf. *Couat*, pp. 1–50; *Susemihl*, I, p. 335 ff.; Parthey, Das Alexandrin. Museum, Berlin, 1838; *Ritschl*, Opusc. I, pp. 1–70, 123–72, 197–237; *Bernhardy*, Gesch. d. griech. Literat. I⁴, pp. 509–43, II 699 ff.; *Wilamo- witz*, Euripides' Heracles, I, p. 121 ff.

a. *Philetas of Cos*, 339–289/5.

Ἄτακτα (Ἄτακτοι γλῶσσαι, Γλῶσσαι). The first attempt at a Homeric lexicon. Cf. Aristarchus, Πρὸς Φιλητᾶν.

On *Philetas* as a poet, vide *Couat*, La Poésie Alexandrine, Paris, 1882, p. 68 ff.; Susemihl, I, p. 174 ff.

b. *Zenodotus of Ephesus*, c. 325–c. 260.

Pupil of Philetas. *First* librarian of Alexandria.

(1) Collection of the works of the *epic* and *lyric* poets. Cf. Schol. Plautinum ; Ritschl, Opusc. l. c.

(2) Γλῶσσαι Ὁμηρικαί (Schol. Od. 3, 444; Schol. Apoll. Rhod. II 1005).

(3) Διόρθωσις (or ἔκδωσις) Ὁμήρου, the first scientific edi- tion of the Iliad and the Odysse. Published shortly before 274 B. C.

On his critical method, cf. *F. A. Wolff*, Proleg. c. 43; *Sengebusch*, Diss.
Hom. I, p. 21 ff.; *Düntzer*, De Zenodoti studiis Homericis, Göttingen,
1848; *Römer*, Ueber die Homerrecension des Zenodot (Münchner Acad.
I, Cl. XVII, pp. 639–722 (1885); *Susemihl*, I, pp. 327–35.

c. Alexander Aetolus, floruit c. 285 B. C.
Collection of the *Greek tragic poets* in the Alexand. Library.
Cf. Ritschl, l. c., pp. 2–4, 199 f.   On his poetry: Meineke, Anal. Alex.
p. 215 ff.; Susemihl, I, pp. 187–90; Couat, p. 105 ff.

d. Lycophron of Chalcis, c. 285 B. C.
(1) Collection of the *comic poets* in the Alexand. Library.
Cf. Ritschl, l. c.
(2) Περὶ κωμῳδίας in at least 11 books.   The oldest work
of its kind.
Cf. *K. Strecker*, De Lycophrone Euphronio Eratosthene comicorum
interpretibus, Greifswald, 1884 (with collection of fragments); *Susemihl*,
I, p. 274. 426.

e. Callimachus of Cyrene, c. 310–c. 240.
Second librarian of Alexandria.   Μέγα βιβλίον, μέγα κακόν.
Chief work: Πίνακες τῶν ἐν πάσῃ παιδείᾳ διαλαμψάν-
των καὶ ὧν συνέγραψαν, 120 books.   On the classifica-
tion and contents of this catalogue :
Cf. *O. Schneider*, Callimachea, II, pp. 297–322; *Wachsmuth*, Philol.
XVI 653 ff.; *Gräfenhan*, II 182 ff.; *Susemihl*, I 337 f.   On C. as a poet cf.
Couat, pp. 111–284; *Susemihl*, I 347–73.

f. Eratosthenes of Cyrene, c. 276–196.
Ὁ φιλόλογος, the first to assume that name.   Cf. Sueton. l. c.
Third librarian of Alexandria.   One of the most versa-
tile and learned scholars of all times.   (ὁ πένταθλος, Βῆτα,
cf. Suidas s. v. ᾽Ερατοσθένης.)
(1) Γεωγραφικά, 3 books.   The first scientific treatment
of the subject.   Cf. *Berger*, Gesch. der wissenschaftl.
Erdkunde bei den Griech. III 57–112, Lpz. 1891.
(2) Περὶ χρονογραφιῶν.   Cf. Diels, Rh. Mus. 31, p. 1 ff.;
Niese, Hermes, XXIII 92 ff.
(3) ᾽Ολυμπιονίκαι.   Cf. Bernhardy, Eratosthenica, p. 247 ff.
(4) Περὶ τῆς ἀρχαίας κωμῳδίας, in at least 12 books.   "A
philological masterpiece."
Cf. Strecker, l. c.; Wilamowitz, Hermes, XXI 597 f.; Bernhardy, l. c.,
p. 203–37, and Susemihl, I 409–28.

g. Aristophanes of Byzantium, c. 257–c. 180.
Librarian, successor of Eratosthenes or Apollonius Rhodius.
The greatest philologist of antiquity.

9

(1) *Invention (?) of accents, punctuation* (acc. to Arcadius, p. 186 ff.).

Cf. Nauck, p. 12 ff.; *Wilamowitz*, l. c., 127 f.; *Susemihl*, I 432, 901 ; *Usener* ap. eundem, II 672.

(2) Κριτικὰ σημεῖα. Cf. Nauck, pp. 15–18. On the symbols themselves see below.

(3) *Editions* with critical signs to—

a. *Homer* (Διόρθωσις Ὁμήρου). Cf. *Wolff*, Proleg. c. 44 ; *Nauck*, l. c., 25–58. Close of the Odyssee, 23, 296. On his method of criticism see Wilamowitz below.

β. *Hesiod*, Theogony (cf. Schol. Theog. 68).

γ. *Alcaeus, Anacreon, Pindar* and perhaps *Simonides* (Dionys. de comp. verb. 26).

δ. *Euripides* (Schol. Or. 714, 1287; Hipp. 172). Cf. Nauck, p. 62 f.

ε. *Aristophanes* (Schol. Av. 1342; Thesm. 162, 917; Ran. 152 f.; Nub. 958). Cf. Nauck, pp. 18, 63–66.

η. *Menander* (?). Cf. his saying: " ὦ Μένανδρε καὶ βίε, πότερος ἄρ' ὑμῶν πότερον ἀπεμιμήσατο ;"

(4) Ὑποθέσεις to Soph. Eur. Arist. and perhaps Aesch. (probably prefixed to his editions). Contents: Argument of the play, its sources, didascalia, aesthetic judgment. The following extant fragments of ὑποθέσεις are probably ultimately based upon those of Aristophanes :

Aeschylus: Persae, Sept. adv. Theb., *Agam.*, Eumen., Prom.

Sophocles: Oed. Col., Philoct., *Aiax,* Oed. Rex (metrical).

Euripides: Hecuba, Orest., *Phoen.*, Medea, *Hyppol.*, Alcest., Androm., Troad. [*Rhesos*], Ion, Iphig. Taur., Bacch., Heracleid., Helena, Hercul. Fur., Cyclops (none extant to Suppl., Iph. Aul., Electra).

Aristophanes: Acharn. I, II (metrical); Equit. I, II, III (met.); Nub. I, II, III, IV (met.), V, VI, VII <VIII, IX, X>; Vesp. I, II (met.); Pax, I, II, III, IV (met.); Aves. I, II, III, IV (met.); Lysist. I, II (met.); Ranae, I, II (met.), <III, IV>; Eccl. I, II (met.); Plut. I, II, III, IV, [V], VI (met.).

Cf. *F. W. Schneidewin*, De hypothesibus tragoed. Graec. Aristoph. Byz. vindicandis (Abh. der Gött. Gesell. der Wiss., Vol. IV, 1853–55); *Nauck*, l. c., p. 255 ff.; *Trendelenburg*, Grammat. Graec. de arte trag. iudiciorum reliquiae, Bonn, 1867.

(5) Παράλληλοι Μενάνδρου τε καὶ ἀφ' ὧν ἔκλεψεν.
(6) Περὶ προσώπων (perhaps the ultimate source of Pollux,
     IV 133–54). Cf. *Nauck*, p. 275 ff.; *Rohde*, De I. P...
     fontibus, Lpz. 1870.
(7) Παροιμίαι (μετρικαὶ and ἄμετροι) in 6 books. Cf. Nauck,
     p. 235–42; Leutsch, Philol. III 566.
(8) Περὶ ἀναλογίας, Nauck, p. 264 ff.
(9) Περὶ τῆς ἀχνυμένης σκυτάλης, a treatise on a passage
     in Archilochus (fragm. 89, 2). Nauck, p. 273 ff.
(10) Λέξεις—Περὶ τῶν ὑποπτευομένων μὴ εἰρῆσθαι τοῖς παλαιοῖς,
     περὶ ὀνομασίας ἡλικιῶν, περὶ συγγενικῶν ὀνομάτων—Ἀττικαὶ λέξεις,
     Λακωνικαὶ γλῶσσαι. The first scientific work on lexicography. About 100 fragments preserved.

Cf. Nauck, l. c., p. 69–190; Rh. Mus. VI 322–51; *Fresenius*, De λέξεων
Aristophanearum et Suetoniarum excerptis Byzantinis, Wiesbaden, 1875;
L. Cohn, Jahrb. f. Philol. Suppl. XII 283–374.

(11) Πρὸς πίνακας Καλλιμάχου. Of this supplement to
     the great catalogue of Callimachus, the extant distribution of the Platonic Dialogues into trilogies (Diog. Laert.
     III 61 f.) formed probably a part.
(12) Κάνονες or lists of 'best authors.' Cf. *Quint*. X 1,
     54: "Apollonius in ordinem a grammaticis datum non
     venit quia Aristarchus atque Aristophanes neminem sui
     temporis in ordinem redegerunt"; vid. also X 1, 59 and
     I 4, 3.

For extant ancient lists cf. *Usener*, Dionysii Halic. librorum de imitatione reliquiae, Bonn, 1889. On the probable character and contents
of these canones, cf. *Ranke*, Vita Aristoph., p. 104 ff.; *Steffen*, De canone
qui dicitur Aristophanis et Aristarchi, Lpz. 1876; *Brzoska*, De canone
decem oratorum, Breslau, 1883; *P. Hartmann*, De canone decem oratorum, Göttingen, 1891, and *Susemihl*, I 445, 484; II 674 f., 694–97.
     On *Aristophanes of Byzantium* in general cf. *A. Nauck*, Aristophanis
Byzantii Fragmenta, Halle, 1848, pp. 338; *Susemihl*, I 428–48; *Wilamowitz*, Eur. Heracles, I 137–53.

h. Aristarchus of Samothrace, 217/5–145/3.

Ὁμηρικός, ὁ κριτικός πάνυ ἄριστος γραμματικός (Schol. Hom. B
     316) ὁ ἀνήρ (Herodianus in Schol. B 153) μάντις (Athen.
     XIV 634). 800 ὑπομνήματα. Difference betw. ὑπομνήματα
     and συγγράμματα. The latter more highly esteemed than
     the former. Cf. Didymus (Schol. B 111): εἰ γὰρ τὰ συγ
     γράμματα τῶν ὑπομνημάτων προτάττομεν.
(1) *Edition of Homer. Two* editions. Cf. Lehrs, p. 23;
     Ludwig, I 17 ff. Cp. Schol. K 397: Ammonius, the

successor of Aristarchus, the author of a treatise "Περὶ τοῦ μὴ γεγονέναι πλείονας (SC. τῶν δύο) ἐκδόσεις τῆς Ἀρισταρχείου διορθώσεως."

(2) Συγγράμματα—Περὶ Ἰλιάδος καὶ Ὀδυσσείας (Schol. I 349), Πρὸς Φιλητᾶν (Schol. A 524, B 111), Πρὸς Κωμανόν (Schol. A 97, B 798, Ω 110), Πρὸς τὸ Ξένωνος παράδοξον (Schol. M 435 and Susemihl, II 149 f.), Περὶ τοῦ ναυσταθμοῦ with a map or διάγραμμα (Κ 53, Μ 258, Ο 449, Λ 166, 807).

On his critical method cf. *Wolff*, Proleg., p. 226 ff.; *Lehrs*, De Aristarchi studiis Homericis, Königsberg, 1882³ (1833¹); *Sengebusch*, Diss. Hom. I 24 ff.; *Ludwig*, Aristarch's Homerische Textkritik nach den Fragmenten des Didymus, 2 vols., Lpz. 1885; *Wilamowitz*, Homer. Unters., p. 383 ff.; Eurip. Heracles, I 154; *Susemihl*, I 451-63; *Jebb*, Homer, Glasgow, 1887, p. 92 ff.

(3) Ὑπομνήματα 'commentaries' and ἐκδόσεις 'editions' with 'critical signs' to—

α. *Hesiod.*

Cf. *Flach*, Jahrb. f. Phil. 109 (1874), p. 815 ff.; 115 (1877), p. 433 ff.; *Waeschke*, De Aristarchi studiis Hesiodiis (Acta Sem. Lips. 1874); *Schömann*, Opusc. II 510 ff.; III 47 ff.

β. Commentary to *Archilochus* (Clem. Strom. I 326 D).

γ. Edition of *Alcaeus* (Hephaest., p. 136) and perhaps of *Anacreon*, certainly a commentary on this poet (Athen. XV 671 f., ἐξηγούμενος).

δ. *Pindar* (edition and commentary). *Feine*, De Aristarcho Pindari interprete (Diss. Ienen. II 253-327); *Horn*, De Aristarchi studiis Pindaricis, Greifswald, 1883; *Susemihl*, I 460 ff.; *Lehrs*, Pindarscholien, Lpz. 1873.

ε. Commentary to *Aeschylus*, at all events to the Λυκοῦργος (Schol. Theocr. X 18). *Ion*, at least to the Ὀμφάλη (Athen. XIV 634 c).

ζ. Commentaries to *Sophocles* (cf. M. Schmidt, Didymi fragmenta, Lpz. 1854, p. 262). *Aristophanes* (*O. Gerhard*, De Aristarcho Aristophanis interprete, Bonn, 1850; *Schneider*, De Aristophanis schol. font., p. 86 f.).

(4) A.'s contributions to *grammar*. The first to distinguish *eight parts of speech*. Cf. Quint. I 4, 20; Schömann, Redetheile, p. 12; Steinthal, l. c.

Plato—1. ὄνομα and 2. ῥῆμα: cf. Classen, l. c., pp. 43-52.

Aristotle (and Theodectes)—1. ὄνομα, 2. ῥῆμα, 3. ἄρθρον 'article,' 4. σύνδεσμός 'conjunction,' ibid., p. 55 ff. According to Dionysius, De comp. verb. 2 (= Quint. I 4), the article was not as yet recognized by these as a separate part of speech, but see Classen, p. 59 f.

Stoics (Chrysippus)—1. ὄνομα, 2. προσηγορία 'appellatio,' 'proper names,' 3. ῥῆμα, 4. σύνδεσμός, 5. ἄρθρον 'article and pronoun,' 6. μεσότητα (πανδέκτης) 'adverb' added by Antipater.

Aristarchus—1. ὄνομα, 2. ῥῆμα, 3. ἀντωνυμία 'pronoun,' 4. ἐπίρρημα 'adverb,' 5. μετοχή 'participle,' 6. ἄρθρον, 7. σύνδεσμός, 8. πρόθεσις 'preposition.'[1]

Cf. Classen; Lersch; Steinthal, vol. II; Schömann, ll. cc.; *R. Schmidt*, Stoicorum grammatica, Halle, 1839; *Th. Rumpel*, Casuslehre, Halle, 1845, pp. 1–70.

(5) *Analogia* (Aristarchus and his school) vs. *Anomalia* (Crates and the Stoics). Cf. Lersch; *Steinthal*, I 357–74; II 71–159.

i. Hermippos ὁ Καλλιμάχειος, of Smyrna.

Βίοι περὶ τῶν ἐν παιδείᾳ λαμψάντων.

Of this voluminous work : περὶ τῶν νομοθετῶν, περὶ δούλων, περὶ τῶν ἔπτα σοφῶν, περὶ Πυθαγόρου, περὶ Ἀριστοτέλους, περὶ Γοργίου, περὶ Ἰσοκράτους, περὶ Ἰσοκράτους μαθητῶν, περὶ ἐνδόξων ἀνδρῶν ἰατρῶν, περὶ μάγων, περὶ τῶν ἀπὸ φιλοσοφίας εἰς τυραννίδας καὶ δυναστείας μεθεστηκότων—generally cited as separate books, formed only so many subdivisions. One of the chief sources of *Diogenes Laertius*, and of *Plutarch's* Lycurgus, Solon, Demosthenes, and indirectly, through the medium of Caecilius, of *Pseudo-Plutarch*, Vitae X oratorum. Cf. *Susemihl*, I 492–95.

k. Apollodorus of Athens (pupil of Aristarchus), flor. c. 150. "Ἀπολλοδώρῳ περὶ πᾶσαν ἱστορίαν ἀνδρὶ δεινῷ" (Ps. Heracl. Alleg. Homer. 7).

(1) Χρονικά in comic trimeters, from the fall of Troy, (1184)–144 B. C. 2d. edition, to about 119 (death of Boethos the Academic mentioned). The inexhaustible

---

[1] The ancients, accustomed to see in Homer the fountain of all wisdom, supposed these *eight* parts of speech to have been well known to him, citing in proof of this the following lines:

Iliad, I 185: αὐτὸς ἰὼν κλισίηνδε τὸ σὸν γέρας ὄφρ' εὖ εἰδῇς.
Iliad, XXII 59: πρὸς δέ με τὸν δύστηνον ἔτι φρονέοντ' ἐλέησον.

storehouse of chronological information throughout antiquity. Calculation of the ἀκμή. Cf. *Diels*, Rh. Mus. 31 (1876), pp. 1–54; also *G. F. Unger*, Philol., 40 (1882), pp. 602–51.

(2) Περὶ τοῦ νεῶν καταλόγου, 12 books. An exhaustive commentary to the Homeric Catalogue of the Ships. Cf. *Niese*, Apollodor's Commentar zum Schiffscataloge als Quelle Strabo's, Rhein. Mus. 32 (1877), pp. 267–307.

(3) Περὶ Σώφρονος, 4 books.

(4) On *Epicharmus*, 10 books.

(5) Περὶ τῶν Ἀθήνησιν ἑταιρῶν.

(6) Περὶ ἐτυμολογιῶν.

(7) Περὶ θεῶν, 24 books. A work of stupendous erudition, freely and extensively pirated by later writers. Cf. *Muenzel*, De Apollodori περὶ θεῶν libris, Bonn, 1883. On A. in general cf. *Susemihl*, II 33–44; Pauly, R. E., I 1300.

l. The first Manual of Mythology, written between 100–50 B. C., the source of *Diodorus, Hyginus, Pseudo-Apollodori* Bibliotheca, *Proclus*.

Cf. *Bethe*, Quaestiones Diodoreae mythographae, Göttingen, 1887, and *Hermes*, 26 (1891), pp. 593–634; *Susemihl*, II 45–52.

m. Ammonius, pupil and successor of Aristarchus.

(1) Περὶ τοῦ μὴ γεγονέναι πλείονας (sc. τῶν δύο) ἐκδόσεις τῆς Ἀριστάρχείου διορθώσεως. See above under Aristarchus.

(2) Περὶ τῶν ὑπὸ Πλάτωνος μετενηνεγμένων ἐξ Ὁμήρου.

(3) Πρὸς Ἀθηνοκλέα σύγγραμμα.

(4) Commentary to *Pindar*.

(5) Κωμῳδούμενοι.

(6) Περὶ τῶν Ἀθήνησιν ἑταιρίδων.

(7) Περὶ προσῳδίας or Περὶ Ἀττικῆς προσῳδίας.

Cf. *Blau*, De Aristarchi discipulis, Jena, 1883; *A. Roemer*, Die Werke der Aristarcheer im Cod. Ven. A, Münch. Acad. II, p. 241 ff. (1875); *La Roche*, Hom. Textkritik, pp. 68–78.

n. Dionysius Thrax of Alexandria, born c. 166 B. C.

(1) Τέχνη γραμματική, the first attempt of its kind and the standard work on the subject for more than 1500 years.

Cf. *Uhlig's* edition, with exhaustive Prolegomena, Lpz. 1884.

On the numerous commentators, among whom *Choe-*

roboscus (6. cent.), *Stephanos* (7. cent.), *Heliodorus, Melampus, Moschopulos* are the most noteworthy.

Cf. *Hoerschelmann*, De Dionysii Thracis interpretibus veteribus I, Lpz. 1874, and especially *Hilgard*, Heidelberg Gymn. Progr., Lpz. 1880.

(2) Commentaries to the *Iliad* and *Odyssee* (28 fragm.). Following Aristarchus, D. regarded Homer as an Athenian.

(3) Commentaries to *Hesiod's Works and Days*.

(4) Πρὸς Κράτητα.

(5) Περὶ ποσοτήτων.

(6) A work on *Rhetoric*.

(7) Μελέται.

Cf. *Mor. Schmidt*, Philol. VII 360–82, VIII 234–53, 510–20; *Susemihl*, II 168–75, 687 f.

o. Didymus Chalcenteros of Alexandria, c. 65 B. C.–c. 10 A. D. Said to have written 3500–4000 books. Χαλκέντερος (Amm. Marcell. 22, 16, 16). Cf. *Quint.* I 8, 19, Didymo, quo nemo plura scripsit, accidisse compertum est, ut cum historiae cuidam tamquam vanae repugnaret, ipsius proferretur liber qui eam continebat. *Athen.* IV 139: καλεῖ δὲ τοῦτον Δημήτριος ὁ Τροιζήνιος βιβλιολάθαν διὰ τὸ πλῆθος ὧν ἐκδέδωκε συγγραμμάτων· ἐστὶ γὰρ τρισχίλια πρὸς τοῖς πεντακοσίοις. *Macrob.* Sat. V 18, 9: grammaticorum facile eruditissimus. 22, 10: grammaticorum omnium … instructissimus. Masterly discussion and estimate of D.'s work by *Wilamowitz*, Eur. Heracl. I 157–68.

(I) *Lexicographical.*

(1) Διεφθορῦια λέξις.

(2) Ἀπορουμένη λέξις, 7 books.

(3) Τροπικὴ λέξις.

(4) Κωμικὴ λέξις. } The chief source of all the lexico-
(5) Τραγικὴ λέξις. } graphical erudition of the ancients preserved in lexica, scholia, Athenaeus, Hesychius, Photius, etc.

(6) Lexicon to Hippocrates (?).

(II) *Didymus as editor of texts and as commentator.*

(1) Περὶ τῆς Ἀριστάρχου διορθώσεως. (Text and commentary to the Homeric poems.) See above.

(2) Commentary to *Hesiod*; cf. Schmidt, p. 299 f.

(3) C. to *Pindar*; id., pp. 214–40.

(4) C. to the *Epinikia* of *Bacchylides*.

(5) C. to *Aeschylus, Sophocles, Euripides* (in part). The extant *vitae* are in all essential details Didymean. Prejudicial and partial criticism of Soph. to the disparagement of Euripides.

(6) C. to *Ion* and perhaps to *Achaeos*; cf. Schmidt, pp. 301–5.

(7) C. to *Cratinus* and *Eupolis*; Schmidt, pp. 307–9.

(8) C. to *Aristophanes*; Schmidt, pp. 246–61; Schneider, De fontibus A. schol., pp. 59–63. [Aristophanes of Byz.—Didymus—Symmachus—extant scholia.]

(9) C. to *Menander* and to *Phrynichus* (Kronos); Schmidt, p. 306 ff.

(10) Editions and Commentaries to *Antiphon, Isaeus, Hypereides, Aeschines* and *Demosthenes*—Schmidt, pp. 310–19—*Isocrates* (?), *Deinarchus* (?).

(11) Edition of *Thucydides*. The extant life by *Marcellinus* (esp. §1–45) was almost entirely taken from Didymus' introduction. Cf. *Susemihl*, II 203 f., note 314.

(12) Ῥητορικὰ ὑπομνήματα, in at least 10 books; Schmidt, p. 321. Exegetical parerga to the *Attic orators*.

(13) Περὶ τοῦ δεκατεῦσαι; Schmidt, p. 317 f.

(III) *Grammatical works*:

(1) Περὶ παθῶν (on inflections); Schmidt, p. 343 ff.

(2) Περὶ ὀρθογραφίας.

(3) Περὶ τῆς παρὰ Ῥωμαίοις ἀναλογίας. Doubtful.

(IV) *Historical, antiquarian, literary treatises*:

(1) Ξένη ἱστορία; cf. Schmidt, pp. 356–63.

(2) *De morte Aeneae;*
(3) *De patria Homeri;* } cf. Schmidt, pp. 384–6.
(4) *On Anacreon and Sappho;*

Cf. *Seneca, Ep.* 88, 37: quatuor milia librorum Didymus grammaticus scripsit ... in his libris de patria Homeri quaeritur, in his de Aeneae morte (matre, MSS) vera, in his libidinosior Anacreon an ebriosior vixerit, in his an Sappho publica fuerit.

(5) Περὶ ποιητῶν; Schmidt, pp. 386–96.

(6) Πρὸς Ἴωνα ἀντεξηγήσεις. (A long extract on the

musical instruments used in lyric poetry preserved by *Athen.* XIV 634 *e.*) Perhaps a part of (5).

(7) Περὶ τῶν ἀξόνων τῶν Σόλωνος ἀντιγραφή πρὸς Ἀσκληπιάδην (Plut. Sol. 1).

(8) *Against Cicero's de Republica*, 6 books. Cf. Amm. Marcell. XXII 16, 16, and Suidas s. v. Τράγκυλλος.

(9) Περὶ παροιμιῶν.

(10) *On the city of Kabassos* and on *Attic demes* (doubtful). Perhaps portions of his commentaries to the Iliad (13, 363) or to the comic poets or to the Attic orators.

Cf. *Mor. Schmidt*, Didymi Chalcenteri grammatici Alexandrini fragmenta, Lpz. 1854; *Ludwig*, l. c.; *Susemihl*, II 195-210, 688 f.

p. Tryphon of Alexandria, son of Ammonius.

A specialist on Greek grammar. A confused list of his numerous works given by *Suidas*, the titles of others cited by Apollonius Dyscolos, Herodianus, Athenaeus.

(1) Περὶ πλεονασμοῦ, περὶ μέτρων, περὶ τρόπων, περὶ σχημάτων.

(2) On the dialects of Greece, on the dialect of Homer and the lyric poets.

(3) Περὶ Ἀττικῆς προσῳδίας, περὶ ὀνομασιῶν, περὶ ὀρθογραφίας καὶ τῶν ἐν αὐτῇ ζητουμένων (= its problems), περὶ Ἑλληνισμοῦ (on idiomatic speech), περὶ ἀρχαίας ἀναγνώσεως (on style).

(4) Περὶ πνευμάτων, περὶ τῆς ἐν μονοσυλλάβοις ἀναλογίας, περὶ τῆς ἐν κλίσεσιν (declensions) ἀναλογίας, περὶ ἄρθρων, περὶ ἀντωνυμιῶν (pronouns), περὶ προσώπων (persons), περὶ μετοχῆς (participle), περὶ προθέσεων (prepositions), περὶ συνδεσμῶν, περὶ ἐπιρρημάτων (adverbs), περὶ ῥημάτων ἐγκλιτικῶν (moods), περὶ ῥημάτων ἀναλογίας βαρυτόνων, περὶ ὀνομάτων συγκριτικῶν (comparison of adjectives), περὶ παθῶν λέξεων (inflections).

(5) Φυτῶν ἱστορία, περὶ ζῴων.

Cf. *A. v. Velsen*, Tryphonis grammatici Alexandrini fragmenta, Berlin, 1854; *Susemihl*, II 210-13, 689.

q. Theon of Alexandria, 1. cent. A. D.

"The Didymus of the Alexandrian poets."

(1) Commentaries to *Lycophron, Theocritos, Callimachus' Αἴτια, Apollonius Rhodius, Nicandros.*

(2) Commentary to the *Odyssee* and perhaps to *Pindar.*

(3) Λέξις κωμική.

(4) Λέξις τραγική (doubtful, but probable).

Cf. *Giese*, De Theone grammatico eiusque reliquiis, Münster, Diss., 1867; *Wilamowitz*, Eur. Heracl. I 156; *Susemihl*, II 216 ff.

3. THE STOICS AS PHILOLOGIANS.
Allegorical exegesis of Homer. Contributions to the Science of Grammar.

Cf. *Gräfenhan*, 1. c., I 440 ff., 505 ff., II 23, III 236: *R. Schmidt*, De Stoicorum grammatica, Halle, 1839; *Steinthal*, 1. c.; *Stricker*, De Stoicorum studiis rhetoricis, Bresl. Abh. I 2 (1886).

4. CRATES OF MALLOS (flor. 168 B. C.) AND THE SCHOOL OF PERGAMUM.
A follower of the Stoics. Passionate opponent of Aristarchus and his school (*Suidas* s. v. Ἀριστάρχου: καὶ Κράτητι τῷ γραμματικῷ πλεῖστα διημιλλήσατο). *Bibaculus* ap. Sueton. de gramm. 11. En. iecur Cratetis. Advocate of ἀνωμαλία vs. ἀναλογία. Cf. the bibliography under Aristarchus and below. Introduced *philological studies into Rome;* cf. Sueton., l. c., p. 100.

(1) *Critical commentary to the Iliad and Odyssee* (Διορθωτικά), with an introduction on the life of Homer.
(2) Ὁμηρικαί. Allegorical commentary.
(3) Commentary to *Hesiod, Works and Days*.
(4) Commentary to *Euripides* (Schol. Orest. 1226, 1686; Phoen. 211; Rhesus, 5, 524 f.; cf. Wilamowitz, Anal. Eurip., p. 157), to *Aristophanes* (Schol. Equit. 631, 793, 693; Vesp. 352, 884; Ran. 294). Cf. *Consbruch*, Zu den Tractaten περὶ κωμῳδίας in Comment. in honor. Studemundi, Strassburg, 1889; *Susemihl*, II 11, note 54.
(5) Περὶ Ἀττικῆς διαλέκτου, in at least 5 books.

Cf. *Wegener*, De aula Attalica, 1836 (antiquated); *Wachsmuth*, De Cratete Mallota, Lpz. 1860, with fragments; id., Philol. XVI 166; Rhein. Mus. 46, pp. 552–56; *Lübbert*, Rhein. Mus. XI 428–43; *Hillscher*, Jahrb. f. Philol. Suppl. N. F. XVIII; *Susemihl*, II 4-12, 703; Introd. to vol. II, p. iv f.; *A. Conze*, Berl. Acad. Sitzungsber. 1884, p. 1259 ff.

b. *Demetrius Magnes* (contemporary of Cicero).
(1) Περὶ συνωνύμων πόλεων.
(2) Περὶ τῶν συνωνύμων ποιητῶν τε καὶ συγγράφεων.
Chapter on *Deinarchus* preserved by *Dionys. Halic.* de Deinarch. One of the chief sources of *Diogenes Laertius*.

Cf. *Nietzsche*, Rhein. Mus. 23, pp. 632–53; 24, pp. 181–228; *Scheurleer*, De D. M., Leiden, 1858; *Maass*, Philol. Unters. III (1880), pp. 23–47; *Susemihl*, I 507 f.

II. THE GRAECO-ROMAN PERIOD.

1. THE POST-ALEXANDRIAN PERIOD.

a. Dionysius of Halicarnassus (flor. end of 1. cent. B. C.).

(1) Epistula ad Ammaeum I.

(2) De compositione verborum.

(3) De oratoribus antiquis (Lysias, Isocrates, Isaeus, Demosth.).

(4) Epistula ad Pompeium.

(5) De Thucydide.

(6) Ad Ammaeum II.

(7) De Dinarcho.

(8) Ars rhetorica.

(9) Veterum censura (περὶ μιμήσεως, bk. II).

Cf. *Fr. Blass*, De D. H. scriptis rhetoricis, Bonn, 1863; *Rössler*, De D. H. scriptis rhetor., Lpz. 1873; *H. Usener*, De H. de imitatione reliquiae, Bonn, 1889; *E. Egger*, l. c. pp. 396–406.

b. Caecilius Calactinus (Friend of Dionysius).

(1) Περὶ τοῦ χαρακτῆρος τῶν δέκα ῥητόρων.
Chief source of Ps. Plut. Vitae X orat. On the canon of the ten orators, see under Aristophanes.

(2) Comparison between Demosth. and Aesch., Demosth. and Cicero.

(3) Περὶ ὕψους (cf. Ps. Longinus, Περὶ ὕψους 1).

(4) Ἐκλογὴ λέξεων κατὰ στοιχεῖον (καλλιρρημοσύνη).

On Dionysius and Caecilius, the most noteworthy representatives of literary criticism in antiquity, cf. *F. Blass*, Gesch. der griech. Beredsamkeit von Alexander bis auf Augustus, Berlin, 1865, pp. 169–221.

c. Διονυσίου ἢ Λογγίνου Περὶ ὕψους (probably composed in the 1 cent. A. D.).

Cf. *Buchenau*, De scriptore libri Περὶ ὕψους, Marb. 1849; *Martens*, De libello Περὶ ὕψους, Bonn, 1877; *Egger*, l. c. pp. 426–39, "Aesthetic Criticism."

d. APOLLONIOS DYSCOLOS, ὁ τεχνικός (2 cent. A. D.).
Founder of scientific syntax. "Σύνταξις ἀναγκαιοτάτη πρὸς ἐξήγησιν τῶν ποιημάτων." "Maximus auctor artis grammaticae" Priscian.

(1) Ὀνοματικόν (declension).

(2) Ῥηματικόν (conjugation).

(3) Περὶ ἀντωνυμίας ⎤

(4) Περὶ ἐπιρρημάτων ⎬ extant   } μέρη τοῦ λόγου.

(5) Περὶ συνδέσμων ⎦

(6) Περὶ συντάξεως, 4 bks., extant.

Cf. *Gräfenhan*, III 109 ff ; *L. Lange*, *Das System der Syntax des A. D.*, Göttingen. 1852; *E. Egger*, A. D., Essai sur l'histoire des théories grammaticales dans l'antiquité, Paris, 1854, pp. 354 ; *Steinthal*, II pp. 220–345; *Opera* ed. R. Schneider et G. Uhlig, Corp. Gramm. Graec. I 1 (1878).

e. AELIUS HERODIANUS (son of A. D.).
The greatest grammarian of antiquity.

(1) Καθολικὴ προσῳδία, 21 bks.
 α. Bk. 1–19—προσῳδίαι, τόνοι.
 β. Bk. 20—χρόνοι ('quantity').
 γ. Bk. 21—On accents, enclitics, diastole, synaloephe.
 Excerpts preserved by *Theodosios* and *Arcadius.*

(2) Περὶ ὀρθογραφίας, περὶ παθῶν, περὶ ὀνομάτων, περὶ κλίσεως ὀνομάτων, περὶ ῥημάτων, περὶ συζυγιῶν ('conjugations'), περὶ βαρβαρισμοῦ, περὶ μονοσυλλάβων. Originals all lost ; contents known through excerpts in later grammarians.

(3) Περὶ μονήρους λέξεως (on peculiar, anomalous grammatical forms). Extant.

Cf. *Aug. Lentz*, Herodiani technici reliquiae, 2 vols., Lpz. 1870 (pp. ccxxviii + 564, vii + 1264, with indexes); *Lehrs*, Herodiani scripta tria, Königsberg, 1848; *Pauly, R. E.*, III 1236–40; *E. Hiller*, Jahrb. f. Philol. (1871) pp. 505–32, 603–29, Quaest. Herodianae, Bonn, 1866.

f. EPITOMATORS, LEXICOGRAPHERS.

 a. *Iuba*, king of Mauretania, "ἁπάντων ἱστορικώτατος βασιλέων," Plut. Sertor. c. 9. Author of the θεατρικὴ ἱστορία, one of the indirect sources of Pollux.
Cf. *Rhode*, De Pollucis fontibus, Lpz. 1870 ; *Bapp*, Lpz. Stud. VIII 110 ff.

 β. *Pamphilus*, Περὶ γλωσσῶν ἤτοι λέξεων (Λειμών). 95 bks.
Epitomized by Vestinus and by *Diogenianos* in 5 bks.

 γ. HERENNIOS PHILON of Byblos (61–141 A. D.).
(1) Περὶ κτήσεως καὶ ἐκλογῆς βιβλίων, 12 bks.
(2) Περὶ πόλεων καὶ οὓς ἑκάστη αὐτῶν ἐνδόξους ἤνεγκεν, in 30 bks. A famous compilation most extensively used by later grammarians, esp. Hesychios and Stephanus Byzantius.
Cf. *Daub*, Jahrb. f. Phil. Suppl. XI 437 ff.

 δ. *Hephaestion* (older contemporary of Athenaeus).
Athen. XV p. 673 e : 'Λαβὼν δὲ παρ' ἐμοῦ ὁ πᾶσιν κλοπὴν ὀνειδίζων Ἡφαιστίων ἐξιδιοποιήσατο τὴν λύσιν.'

Chief work: Περὶ μέτρων. 48 bks. (lost). His own epitome ('Εγχειρίδιον περὶ μέτρων) in 1 bk. became the standard school-book throughout later antiquity and the Middle Ages.

Edited by Westphal (Script. metric. vol. I, Teubner). Cf. the same, Metrik der Griechen vol. I, introduction.

ε. Aelius Dionysius and Pausanias, 'Αττικισταί.

Cf. Rindfleisch, De P. et D. lexicis rhetoricis, Königsberg, 1866.

ζ. Valerius Harpocration (2 cent.).

Λέξεις τῶν δέκα ῥητόρων.

Edited by Dindorf, Oxford, 1853, 3 vols. Cf. Boysen, De Harpocratiae fontibus, Kiel, 1876.

η. Julius Pollux (Πολυδεύκης) of Naucratis.

'Ονομαστικόν in 10 bks. ed. Dindorf, 5 vols. 1824. Cf. Rhode, l. c.

θ. Cassius Longinus (†270-275).

'Βιβλιοθήκη ἔμψυχος καὶ περιπατοῦν μουσεῖον,' Eunapios. ' Φιλόλογος μὲν ὁ Λογγῖνος, φιλόσοφος δὲ μηδαμῶς,' Porphyrius. Pupil of Plotinus, teacher of Porphyrius. ὁ κριτικός (Suidas s. v. Φρόντων).

(1) Φιλόλογοι ὁμιλίαι at least 21 bks.; fragm.

(2) 'Αττικῶν λέξεων ἐκδόσεις.

(3) 'Απορήματα 'Ομηρικά, Προβλήματα 'Ομήρου καὶ λύσεις, εἰ φιλόσοφος "Ομηρος. } lost.

(4) Rhetoric (ἀφορμαὶ λόγου) discovered by Ruhnken amid the Rhetoric of Apsines; cf. Walz Rhet. Graec. IX p. xxiii ff.

(5) [Περὶ ὕψους] falsely ascribed to Longinus; cf. above.

Cf. D. Ruhnken, De vita et scriptis Longini, 1776; E. Egger, pp. 475-84.

LIST OF THE MOST IMPORTANT EXTANT SCHOLIA.

Cf. E. Hübner, Encyclopaedie, pp. 37-40³.

1. Homer.

Subscriptio in the cod. Ven. A: Παράκειται τὰ 'Αριστονίκου σημεῖα καὶ Διδύμου περὶ 'Αρισταρχείου διορθώσεως, τινὰ δὲ καὶ ἐκ τῆς 'Ιλιαδῆς προσῳδίας 'Ηρωδιανοῦ καὶ ἐκ τῶν Νικάνορος περὶ στιγμῆς. "Viermänner Scholien," cf. above.

Cf. Ludwig, l. c., Friedländer, Aristonicus; id. Nicanor; Fabricius, Bibl. Gr. I pp. 440-56 (index auctorum).

2. *Aristophanes.*
Subscriptio to the Clouds and Wasps: κεκώλισται ἐκ τοῦ
Ἡλιοδώρου, παραγέγραπται ἐκ τοῦ Φαεινοῦ καὶ Συμμάχου καὶ
ἄλλων τινῶν.
Cf. O. *Schneider*, De Veterum in Arist. scholiorum fontibus, 1838 ;
Wilamowitz. Eur. Hercul. I 179-88 ; Fabricius II, pp. 392-404 (index
auctorum).

3. *Apollonius Rhodius.*
Subscriptio in the Cod. Mediceus: Παράκειται τὰ σχόλια ἐκ τῶν
Λουκίλλου Ταρραίου καὶ Σοφοκλέους καὶ Θέωνος.
Cf. *Weichert*, Apollon. Rhod. p. 400 ff.; *Bernhardy*, Griech. Literat. II
1 p. 370 ff.; *Susemihl*, I 662, II 46, 686.

4. *Pindar.* Cf. K. Lehrs, Die Pindarscholien, Lpz. 1863;
Fabricius II 81-4.

5. *Aeschylus.* J. Richter, De Aesch. Soph. Eur. interpretibus
Graecis, Berlin, 1839.

6. *Sophocles.* Bernhardy, l. c. II 2, p. 378 ff.

7. *Euripides.* Bernhardy, l. c. II 2, p. 498 ff. ; ed. E. Schwartz,
2 vols. 1891.

8. *Theocritos.* Ed. Ahrens.

9. *Lycophron.* (I. Tzetzes.)

10. *Plato.* L. Cohn, J. J. Suppl. 13, 773. Th. Mettauer, De
Platonis scholiorum fontibus, Zürich, 1880 (pp. 122).

11. *Aristotle.* Commentaries of Alexander of Aphrodisias,
Simplicius, Philoponus.

CRITICAL SIGNS (Σεμεῖα, notae).
Cf. Reifferscheid, Suetonii Reliquiae, pp. 137-44.

Ὄβελος (—).—‘πρὸς τὰ νόθα καὶ ἀθετούμενα. Legendary origin of
name, l. c. p. 138.
Διπλῆ ἀπεριστικός καθαρά (>—).—‘παράκειται: 1. πρὸς τὴν ἅπαξ
εἰρημένην λέξιν ; 2. πρὸς τὴν τοῦ ποιητοῦ συνήθειαν (inconsistency) ;
3. πρὸς τοὺς λέγοντας, μὴ εἶναι τοῦ αὐτοῦ ποιητοῦ Ἰλιάδα καὶ Ὀδύσσειαν
(χωρίζοντες) ; 4. πρὸς τὰς τῶν παλαιῶν ἱστορίας ; 5. πρὸς τὰς τῶν νέων
ἐνδοχάς ; 6. πρὸς τὴν Ἀττικὴν σύνταξιν ; 7. πρὸς τὴν πολύσημον λέξιν.’
‘ Usus est ea in multis *Aristarchus*, nunc ea quae praeter con-
suetudinem tam vitae nostrae quam ipsius poetae apud eum
invenirentur adnotans, nunc proprias ipsius figuras, interdum
ea in quibus copiosus est rursus quae semel apud eum ponerentur. Similiter in nostris auctoribus *Probus.*’ ‘ Primus Leogoras

22

Syracusanus apposuit Homericis versibus ad separationem
Olympi a caelo.'

Διπλῆ περιεστιγμένη (>+).—'πρὸς τὰς γραφὰς τὰς Ζηνοδοτείους καὶ
Κράτητος καὶ αὐτοῦ Ἀριστάρχου καὶ τὰς διορθώσεις αὐτοῦ.'

Ἀστερίσκος καθ' ἑαυτόν (✳).—'πρὸς τοὺς αὐτοὺς στίχους οἳ κεῖνται ἐν
ἄλλοις μέρεσιν τῆς ποιήσεως, καὶ ὀρθῶς ἔχοντες φέρονται, σημαίνων ὅτι οὗτοι
καὶ ἀλλαχοῦ εἴρηνται.' ' Aristophanes apponebat illis locis quibus
sensus deesset, Aristarchus autem ad eos [versus] qui hoc puta
loco [recte] positi erant, cum aliis scilicet non recte ponerentur,
item Probus et antiqui nostri.' Cf. however schol. γ 71.

Ἀστερίσκος μετ' ὀβελοῦ (✳ —).—'ἔνθα εἰσὶ μὲν τὰ ἔπη τοῦ ποιητοῦ
οὐ καλῶς δὲ κεῖνται, ἀλλ' ἐν ἄλλῳ.' ' Propria est nota Aristarchi,
utebatur autem ea in his versibus qui non suo loco positi sunt,
item Probus et antiqui nostri.' Cf. e. g. A 195.

Ἀντίσιγμα (ↄ).—'πρὸς τοὺς ἐνηλλαγμένους τόπους καὶ μὴ συνᾴδοντας.'
' Ponebatur ad eos versus quorum ordo permutandus erat.'

Ἀντίσιγμα περιεστιγμένον (ↄ˙).—'ὅταν δύο ὦσι διάνοιαι τὸ αὐτὸ
σημαινούσαι (ταυτολογεῖ), τοῦ ποιητοῦ γεγραφότος ἀμφυτέρας, ὅπως τὴν
ἑτέραν ἕληται,' σίγμα—Aristoph. στιγμή—Aristarch. Cf. B 192.

Κεραύνιον (T)—Rare.—'δηλοῖ πολλὰς ζητήσεις πρὸς ταῖς προειρημέναις.'
' Ponitur quotiens multi versus improbantur ne per singulos
obelentur.'

Ancient authorities : Aristonicus (see above), Diogenianos (?) περὶ τῶν
ἐν τοῖς βιβλίοις σημείων (Suid.), Diog. Laert. III 65, Suetonius = Isidorus,
Origg. I 21 ff., de notis scripturarum. See below. Anecd. Roman
Osann, Anecd. Venetum. ed. Villoison, Anecd. Paris. ed. Cramer (all col-
lected in Reifferscheid l. c.).
Modern treatises: Gräfenhan II 92 f.; Sengebusch, Hom. Diss. I p. 22 ff.;
Nauck, Aristoph. Byzant. p. 17 ff.; Ludwig, I 20 ff.; Susemihl, I p. 432 ff.;
and H. Schrader, De notatione critica a veteribus grammaticis in poetis
scaenicis adhibita, Bonn, 1863.

2. ROMAN PERIOD.

Bibliography: Suetonius, de grammat. et rhetor.; W. H. D. Suringar,
Historia Critica scholiastarum Latinorum, 3 vols., Leyden, 1835 ; Gräfenhan, II p. 261 ff. IV ; Teuffel-Schwabe, Röm. Literat. 2 vols. 1890⁵
< T. S.> § 41 ; H. Nettleship, Journ. of Phil. XV p. 189 ff.

a. L. Accius (170–c. 86).

Didascalica (cf. Aristotle's Διδασκαλίαι). A history of
Greek and Roman poetry, with special reference to the
drama. Written chiefly in Sotadean verse. Cf. T. S.
§134, 7, and 94, 2. G. Ribbeck, Röm. Dichtkunst,
I 267.

b. L. Aelius Praeconinus Stilo (flor. c. 100 B. C.).
The *first* Roman philologian, teacher of Cicero and Varro.
Cic. Brut. 205: eruditissimus et Graecis litteris et
Latinis antiquitatisque nostrae et in inventis rebus et in
actis scriptorumque veterum litterate peritus, quam
scientiam Varro noster acceptam ab illo. *Varro ap.
Gell. N. A.*, I 18, 2: litteris ornatissimus memoria nostra,
id. X 21, 2 doctissimus eorum temporum.

(1) Commentaries to *Carmina Saliorum*, cf. *Suringar*
I 26. f.

(2) Interpretation of the *XII tables. Suringar* I p.
39 ff.

(3) Edition of *Plautus* with critical signs.

Gell. N. A., III 3, 12: L. Aelius XXV (comoe-
dias) eius (Plauti) esse solas existimavit ; *Quint.*
X 1, 99, " Licet Varro Musas, Aeli Stilonis sen-
tentia, Plautino dicat sermone locuturas fuisse, si
Latine loqui vellent." Cf. *Ritschl, Parerga* 91 ff.,
126 f., 238, 366.

(4) Contributions to *etymology* and *grammar*.

Cf. T. S. § 148, 1. *F. Mentz*, De L. Aelio Stilone, Diss. Ienens. IV 1.

c. M. Tullius Cicero, 106–43.

(1) Literary or aesthetic criticism.

Cf. *Ch. Causeret*, Sur la langue de la rhétorique et de la critique litté-
raire en Cic., Paris, 1887 ; *I. Kubik*, De Cic. poetarum lat. studiis, Diss.
Vindob. I 237 ff.

(2) Edition of *Lucretius*.

Cf. *Munro*, Lucretius, vol. II p. 2 ff. ; T. S. § 203, 2.

d. C. Iulius Caesar, 100–44.
De analogia (Suet. Caes. c. 56). .

Cf. *F. Schlitte*, De C. Iulio Caesare grammatico, Halle, 1865.

e. M. TERENTIUS VARRO *Reatinus*, 116–27.
'Vir Romanorum eruditissimus' (Quint. X 1, 95). 'Vir
doctissimus undicumque Varro, qui tam multa legit
ut aliquid ei scribere vacasse miremur, tam multa scripsit (620 bks.) quam vix quemquam legere potuisse cre-
damus' (Augustin. Civ. Dei. 6, 2). *Plut. Rom.* 12 ἄνδρα
Ῥωμαίων ἐν ἱστορίᾳ βιβλιακώτατον. Esp. *Cic. Acad. post.*
I, 9.

Cf. *Ritschl*, Die Schriftstellerei des Varro, *Opusc.* III 419–505, *Parerga*,
p. 70 ff.; T. S. §166 f.

(1) *Antiquitatum libri* XLI.

(3) Annalium libri III—De vita populi Romani (cp. Dicaearchos Βίος 'Ελλάδος); De gente populi Romani, in 4 bks. (43 B. C.); de familiis Troianis; Aetia (cp. Αἴτια of Callimachus); rerum urbanarum libri III; Tribuum liber.

(3) De bibliothecis libri III; de proprietate scriptorum; *de poetis; de poematis;* de lectionibus; de compositione saturarum; de originibus scaenicis; de scaenicis actionibus; de actis scaenicis (Didascalica); de personis (masks); de descriptionibus; *quaestiones Plautinae; de comoediis Plautinis.*

(4) Disciplinarum libri IX (Artes liberales: 1. grammatica; 2. dialectica; 3. rhetorica; 4. geometria; 5. arithmetica; 6. astrologia; 7. musica; 8. medicina; 9. architectura).

(5). *De Lingua Latina*, XXV lbb. (V–X extant).
V–XXV, dedicated to Cicero, hence published before 43 B. C. *Contents:* Bk. I (introd.); bk. II–VII (etymology), VIII–XVI (inflection, analogy and anomaly), XVII–XXV (syntax).

Cf. O. Spengel's edition, 1885, Berlin.

(6). De sermone Latino libb. V; de similitudine verborum libb. III (analogy); de utilitate sermonis; περὶ χαρακτήρων (? = descriptiones); de antiquitate litterarum; de origine linguae latinae.

Cf. *Wilmanns*, de M. T. V. libris grammaticis, Berlin, 1864.

f. Ateius Praetextatus Philologus († c. 29 B. C.) Cf. Suet. de gramm., 10 T. S., §211.

g. Noted philologists and grammarians of the Empire. First Century.

1. *Asconius Pedianus*, Commentator of Cicero's speeches.

Cf. T. S., §295; *Madvig*, de Q. Ascon. Ped. . . . in Cic. oratt. commentariis, Kopenhagen, 1828.

2. *Fenestella* († 19 A. D.); 'diligentissimus scriptor,' Lactantius. *Annales* in at least 22 bks. A repository of information for later writers.

Fragments ap. H. Peter, Fragm. histor. 272; T. S., §259.

25

3. *M. Valerius Flaccus* (floruit 10 B. C.)
   a. De verborum significatu. Second half preserved in a
mutilated *epitome* of *Festus*, who in turn was epitomized
by *Paulus.* Inexhaustible fountain of information on
Roman antiquities and archaic Latin.

Edited by E. Thewrewk, 1891.

   β. *Fasti,* partly preserved (C. I. L. I 295). Used by
Ovid.

Cf. *H. Winther,* De fastis V. F. ab Ovidio adhibitis, Berlin, 1885.
Cf. T. S., §261; *Hübner,* Grundr. der lat. Lit., §83 (1876³); *H. Nettle-ship,* Lectures and Essays, 201 ff.

4. *M. Valerius Probus Berytius* (flor. 80 A. D.)
The greatest Roman philologist. 'Nec Probum timeto'
(Mart. 3, 2, 12).
   (1). *Editions with critical signs* (cf. Suetonii reliq., p.
138 R).
   a. *Virgil* (Suringar, II, p. 8 ff.; Kübler, De P. comment.
Verg., Berl. 1881).
   β. *Horace, Lucretius, Terence.*
   (2). De notis singularibus, ed. Mommsen, *Gram. Lat.*
IV 271.

Cf. I. Steub, De Probis grammaticis, Jena, 1871; T. S., §300 f.

5. *C. Plinius Secundus,* the Elder, 23–79.
   (1). Libri *dubii sermonis* (cf. Pliny, Ep. III 5, 1).
   (2). De *grammatica* (Pliny, N. H., praef. 28).

6. *Fabius Quintilianus* of Calagurris in Spain, c. 35–95.
Literary criticism, esp. in bk. X of the Institutio Ora-
toria. Pupil of *Remmius Palaemon* (T. S., §282) and
teacher of *Pliny* the Younger and *Cornelius Tacitus* (cf.
Liebert, de doctrina Taciti, Würzburg, 1868, p. 4 ff.).

7. *C. Suetonius Tranquillus,* 75–160.

Cf. Suidas s. v. Τράγκυλλος. Cf. *Reifferscheid,* Suetoni reliquiae praeter
Caesares, Lpz. 1860 (fragments, pp. 3–360; quaest. Suetonianae, pp. 363–
538; indexes, pp. 541–65).

   (1). *De viris illustribus* (de poetis, de oratoribus, de
historicis, de philosophis, de grammaticis et rhetoribus).
   (2). Περὶ τῶν ἐν τοῖς βιβλίοις σημείων βιβλίον ά (Suidas) = de
notis (cf. above).
   (3). *Pratum* (de anno Romanorum, Reiff., pp. 149–92;
de naturis rerum, pp. 193–265; de genere vestium, pp.

26

266–72; περὶ δυσφήμων λέξεων ἤτοι βλασφημιῶν καὶ πόθεν ἑκάστη (cf. Etym. Magnum. s. v. Ἀρχολίπαρος and Eust. ad Iliad. II 234, VIII 488). *Verborum differentiae*, pp. 274–96.

(4). *Ludicra historia* (περὶ τῶν παρ' Ἕλλησι παιδιῶν), pp. 322–45.

(5). De lusibus puerorum.

(6). De institutione officiorum.

(7). Περὶ τῆς Κικέρωνος πολιτείας; ἀντιλέγει δὲ τῷ Διδύμῳ (see above).

Second Century.

Aemilius Asper (T. S., §482, 3), Flavius Caper (T. S., §343, 3), Q. Terentius Scaurus (T. S., §352, 1), Arruntius Celsus (T. S., §357, 3), Iulius Romanus (T. S., §379, 1), *A. Gellius*, Noctes Atticae (T. S., §365).

Third Century.

Censorinus, de die natali (T. S., §379).

Fourth Century.

1. *Nonius Marcellus*, Compendiosa Doctrina (T. S. 404*).
2. Charisius and Diomedes (T. S., §419).
3. Marius Victorinus (T. S., §408, 1).
4. *Aelius Donatus* (floruit c. 350).
   (1). Grammatica.
   (2). *Commentary to Terence.*
   (3). *Commentary to Virgil.* Cf. Gräfenhan, IV 107 ff.; Suringar, I 78–86, II 31–59; T. S., §409, 3 f.
5. Maurus *Servius* Honoratus.
   Commentary to *Virgil.* Cf. Suringar, II 59–92; T. S., §431.

Fifth Century.

1. *Macrobius*, Saturnalia. T. S., §444.
2. Isidorus. T. S., §496.
3. *Priscian of Caesarea.*

   Institutiones grammaticae, 18 bks. The most important and exhaustive work on Latin grammar made by the Romans. An inexhaustible fountain of information for grammatical theories of earlier writers, especially Greek, now lost. The standard work on the subject throughout the Middle Ages. About 1000 MSS known.

Cf. T. S., §481, and Encyclop. Britan. s. v.

III. The Middle Ages.

1. The Byzantian Period.

K. Krumbacher, Grundriss der byzantinischen Literatur (I. Müller's Handbuch der class. Alterthumswissenschaft, vol. IX, 1), Characteristic of the period, pp. 214–17; Wilamowitz, Eur. Heracles, I 193–219.

a. Hesychios of Alexandria.

Lexicon (Γλῶσσαι). Based upon the Περιεργοπένητες of Diogenianos.

b. Hesychios Illustris of Miletus (6. cent.)

'Ονοματόλογος ἢ πίναξ τῶν ἐν παιδείᾳ ὀνομαστῶν. (Only preserved in excerpts.) (Chief sources: Aelius Dionysius' Μουσικὴ ἱστορία, and Herennios Philon.) Cf. Kr., p. 110 ff.

c. Photios, c. 820–c. 891.

(1). Βιβλιοθήκη or Μυριόβιβλον (written before 857). Contains the excerpts and criticisms of 280 books read by the author while ambassador to Assyria.

(2). Λέξεων συναγωγή (based on Harpocration, Diogenianos, 'Αττικῶν ὀνομάτων λόγοι of Aelius Dionysius, Pausanias' Λέξικον κατὰ στοιχεῖον, Platonic lexicon of Timaeus, and Boethos, Homeric lexica of Apion, Heliodorus and Apollonius.

Cf. Kr., pp. 223–33; Fabricius, Bibl. Gr. X 678–775.

d. Constantinos Porphyrogennetos, emperor (912–59, resp. 945). *Encyclopaedia of History*, arranged according to subject-matter (*e. g.* Περὶ Πρεσβειῶν, περὶ ἐπιβουλῶν κατὰ βασιλέων γεγονυιῶν, περὶ στρατηγημάτων, περὶ δημηγοριῶν), with the original chapters of earlier historians bearing upon the respective subjects. Cf. Kr., pp. 59–69.

e. Suidas.

Lexicon (compiled not later than 976 A. D. First cited by Eustathius). A colossal monument of erudition, notwithstanding many instances of gross carelessness. The sources of Suidas have as yet been determined with only partial accuracy, but he seems to have derived, though generally only at second hand, the bulk of his material from the following :

    a. Lexica : Harpocration, Aelius Dionysius, Pausanias, Helladios, Eudemos, Γλῶσσαι to Herodotus, and above all, *Hesychios* (cf. Suidas s. v. 'οὗ ἐπιτομή ἐστι τοῦτο τὸ βιβλίον'), Lexica to Euripides, Menander, Callimachus.

β. *Scholia and Commentaries to:* Aristophanes (in a more complete form than the extant scholia), Sophocles (Oed. Col., Oed. Tyr., Aiax), *Homer* (similar to those of the Venetus B), Thucydides, Philoponus and Alexander of Aphrodisias to Aristotle.

γ. *Histories:* Herodotus, Thucydides, Xenophon's Anabasis, Polybius, Josephus, Arrian, Aelian (probably from Constantinos' Encyclopaedia), Lucian.

δ. *Literary and Biographical material:* Hesychios (see above), *Athenaeus* (bks. I and II in their unepitomized form). Whether the colossal work of *Philon of Byblos* (see above) was known to Suidas at first hand is very doubtful. *Strabo* is completely ignored.

Cf. *Fabricius*, Bibliotheca Graeca, VI 389-595 ; *G. Bernhardy*, Suidae Lexicon, I, Prolegomena, pp. 25–95 ; *Kr.*, pp. 261–67.

f. Johannes Tzetzes, c. 1110–c. 1185.

(1). Βίβλος ἱστοριῶν (Chiliades), in 12,674 political verses.

(2). *Allegories to the Iliad and Odyssee,* 10,000 verses.

'Ο ˚Ομηρος ὁ πάνσοφος, ἡ θάλασσα τῶν λόγων. Homeric mythology interpreted allegorically after the manner of Euhemerus.

(3). Commentary to the Iliad.

(4). Carmina Iliaca (Antehomerica, Homerica, Posthomerica).

(5). Scholia to Hesiod's Works and Days, and the Shield of Heracles.

(6). Scholia to Aristophanes' Plutos, Clouds, Frogs, and arguments to the Knights and Birds.

Cf. Ritschl (Keil), Opusc. I 1-172, 197-237.

(7). Scholia to *Lycophron's Alexandra.*
Invaluable as the only extant key to the understanding of this enigmatical poem.

(8). Scholia to the Halieutica of *Oppian,* and the Theriaca and Alexipharmaca of *Nicandros.*

(9). Epitome of the Rhetoric of *Hermogenes.*

(10). Περὶ τῶν ἐν τοῖς στίχοις μέτρων ἁπάντων, στίχοι περὶ διαφορᾶς ποιητῶν, ἴαμβοι τεχνικοί περὶ κωμῳδίας, περὶ τραγικῆς ποιήσεως.

Cf. Kr., pp. 245–43.

g. Eustathios, Archbishop of Thessalonice (floruit 1175).

(1). *Commentary to the Iliad and Odyssee.*
Invaluable repository of ancient learning.

Principal sources: Homeric scholia, Athenaeus, Strabo, Stephanus of Byzantium, *Aristophanes* of Byzantium, Heraclides of Miletos, and two works by *Suetonius* (written in Greek); Aelios Dionysius, Pausanias, and rhetorical lexica, Suidas and the Etymologicum Magnum.

(2). Paraphrase and scholia to *Dionysius Periegetes.*

(3). Commentary to Pindar (only a valuable preface preserved).

Cf. Kr., pp. 242–47; Fabricius, l. c., I 457–501.

h. Maximus Planudes, 1260–1310.

(1). Περὶ γραμματικῆς, περὶ συντάξεως.

(2). Scholia to Theocritos and Hermogenes.

(3). Συναγωγή ἐκλεγεῖσα ἀπὸ διαφόρων βιβλίων, containing excerpts, e. g., from Plato, Aristotle, Strabo, Pausanias, Dio Cassius.

(4). *Anthologia Planudea.*
The *Anthologia Palatina* was not discovered till 1607 by Salmasius. Grotius' celebrated translation is based upon the Planudean collection.

(5). *Translations from Latin into Greek.*

a. Caesar, De bello Gallico.

β. Cicero, Somnium Scipionis.

γ. Disticha Catonis.

δ. Ovid, Metamorphoses.

ε. *Ovid, Heroides.* On the basis of a very valuable MS now lost.

Cf. A. G. in Calvary's Berl. Stud. VIII 3, pp. 90 (1888).

ζ. *Boethius,* De consolatione philosophiae (his masterpiece).

Cf. *M. Treu,* Comment. to Planudis Epistulae, Breslau, 1890; A. G. in Proc. Am. Philol. Assoc. XX, p. 6 ff.; Kr., p. 248 f.

i. Manuel Moschopulos (pupil of Planudes).

a. Ἐρωτήματα γραμματικά. Of vast pedagogical influence toward the spread of Greek studies in the Renaissance. The famous grammar of *Melanchthon* is essentially a reproduction of the Ἐρωτήματα. Cf. L. Voltz, Jahrb. f. Phil., 139 (1889), p. 579 ff.

β. *Scholia* to the Iliad, bks. I and II. Hesiod, Pindar's Olymp. Odes, Euripides, Theocritos.

Cf. *K. Hartfelder*, Philipp Melanchthon, Berl. 1889, p. 225; M. Treu, l. c., pp. 208–12; Kr., p. 251 f.

k. Thomas Magister (contemporary of *i*).

(1). Ἐκλογὴ ὀνομάτων καὶ ῥημάτων Ἀττικῶν.

(2). Scholia to Aesch., Soph., Eurip., to three comedies of Aristophanes.

Cf. *Fr. Ritschl*, Thomae Magistri ecloga, Halle, 1832, with exhaustive Prolegomena; Kr., p. 253 f.

l. Demetrius Triklinios (beginning of 14. cent.)
The foremost text critic among Byzantian philologians. Notable contributions to Greek versification.

Cf. *Wilamowitz*, Eur. Heracl. I 194 f.; Hermes, 25, pp. 161–70.

(1). Scholia to *Pindar*, and two metrical dissertations, and one of the extant paraphrases to Pindar (Lehrs, Pindarscholien, p. 78).

(2). Text edition, with scholia to *Sophocles*.

(3). Scholia to five plays of *Aeschylos* (except Choephoroe and Supplices). Preserved in Triklinios' own handwriting.

(4). Scholia to Hesiod, Aristophanes and Theocritos. Cf. Kr., p. 256 ff.

2. THE MIDDLE AGES IN W. EUROPE.
Copying of MSS in monasteries.

Cf. *A. H. L. Heeren*, Gesch. des Stud. der class. Literat. seit d. Wiederaufleben d. Wissensch., vol. I, Introduct., pp. 1–308; *W. Wattenbach*, Schriftwesen im Mittelalter, 1875²; Anleit. z. griech. Palaeographie, 1877²; Anleit. z. lat. Palaeog. 1886⁴; *Th. Birt*, Das antike Buchwesen, Berlin, 1882; *A. Ebert*, Allgem. Gesch. der Liter. des Mittelalters, 3 vols., 1887²; Bernhardy, I⁴, p. 716 ff.; E. Hübner, Encyclop., pp. 56–64.

LIST OF SOME OF THE OLDEST CLASSICAL MSS.

1. *Greek.*

a. Fragments of Euripides' Antiope and Plato's Phaedo, 250 B. C. (Flinder's Petrie Papyri, ed. Mahaffy, Dublin Acad. 1890.) The oldest specimens of a classical text known.

b. A few lines of the *XI. Iliad* (ante-Aristarchean and non-Zenodotean), 240 B. C. Most of the following dates are only conjectural.

c. Louvre fragments of *Euripides,* 2. cent. B. C.

d. Alcman, 2.–1. cent. B. C.

e. Iliad fragments (Banks, Harris), 2. cent. B. C.

f. Papyri from *Herculaneum,* 79 A. D. (Epicurus, Philodemos, etc.)

g. Aristotle, 'Aθηναίων Πολιτεία, \
h. Herodas, Mimiambi. } 1.–2. cent. A. D.

i. Four speeches of *Hypereides,* 150 A. D.

k. Berlin fragm. of the *Melanippe* of *Euripides,* 3.–4. cent.

l. Papyrus fragm. of *Isocrates,* 4. cent.

m. Cod. Ambrosianus of the *Iliad.* \
n. Cod. Vaticanus of *Cassius Dio.* \
o. Euripides' *Phaeton* and *Menander,* fragm. } 5.–6. cent. \
p. Fragm. of *Arist. Birds.*

2. *Latin.*

a. Fragm. of Seneca, 1. cent.

b. Seven oldest MSS of *Virgil,* 3.–5. cent.

c. Fragm. of *Sallust's* Historiae, 3.–4. cent.

d. Codex Bembinus of *Terence,* 4.–5. cent.

e. Codex Sessorianus of *Pliny,* N. H. 23–25, 5. cent.

f. Codex Puteaneus of Livy, 6.–7. cent.

g. Palimpsesti.

α. Iuvenal and Persius, fragm. in cod. Vatic., 3.–4. cent.

β. Codex Veronensis and cod. Vaticanus of *Livy.*

γ. *Lucan* (Vienna, Naples, Rome), 4. cent.

δ. *Cicero's De republica,* 4.–5. cent.

ε. Cicero's Speeches in Verrem, fragm. in cod. Vatic., 5. cent.

ζ. *Plautus* (cod. Ambrosianus), 5.–6. cent.

η. Gellius and Seneca, fragm., 5.–6. cent.

θ. *Fronto,* fragm., 4.–6. cent.

ι. Livy, fragm. (Vienna), 5. cent.

Cf. E. Hübner, Encyclop., pp. 45–54.

IV. THE REVIVAL OF LEARNING IN ITALY.

Cf. *G. Voigt,* Die Wiederbelebung des class. Alterthums, 2 vols., Berlin, 1881²; *J. A. Symonds,* Renaissance in Italy (vol. II. The Revival of Learning), 1877; *I. Burkhardt,* Die Cultur der Renaissance in Italien, 1885⁵; D. Comparetti, Virgilio nel medio evo, 2 vols., Livorno, 1872; F. A. Eckstein, Nomenclator philologorum, Lpz. 1871, pp. 656: W. Pökel, Philolog. Schriftstellerlexicon, Lpz. 1882.

(A). GREEK IMMIGRANTS.

Cf. H. Hodius, De Graecis illustr. linguae Graecae litterarumque humaniorum instauratoribus, London, 1742; Bernhardy, I⁴ 730 ff.

(1). *Manuel Chrysoloras*, 1350–1415.

In Florence in 1396, thereafter in Pavia, Venice, Rome. Died in Germany. Niccoli, Bruni, Marsuppini, Traversari among his pupils.

   a. Ἐρωτήματα τῆς Ἑλληνικῆς.

   b. Verbatim translation of Plato's Republic.

Cf. Voigt, I 225–35; Symonds, p. 108 ff.

(2). *Georgios Gemisthios Plethon*, 1355–1452.

Famous Platonist. Voigt, II 119–22; Symonds, pp. 198–210.

(3). *Bessarion*, 1403–72.

Pupil of Plethon. Famous library of 800 MSS bequeathed to Venice (the foundation of the St. Marcus Library). *Translator* of *Arist. Metaphysics, Xenophon's* Memorabilia.

For a list of his works cf. Fabricius, X. In general: Voigt, II 124–33; Symonds, p. 247 ff.; H. Vast, Le Cardinal Bessarion, Paris, 1879.

(4). *Theodorus Gaza*, c. 1400–c. 1478.

   a. Γραμματικὴ εἰσαγωγή.

   b. Celebrated translations of: *Aristotle*, Theophrastus, de plantis, Aelian, Dionysius, De compositione verborum. Cicero, Cato and Laelius into Greek.

Cf. Hody, pp. 55–101; Voigt, II, p. 145 ff.; *L. Stein*, Archiv f. Gesch. der Philosophie, II 3, pp. 426–58.

(5). *Demetrius Chalcondylas*, 1428–1510.

   a. Edition of *Homer* (ed. pr. 1488), *Isocrates, Suidas.*

   b. Ἐρωτήματα.

Cf. Hody, pp. 211–26; Voigt, I 442.

(6). *Constantinos Lascaris* († after 1500).

   a. Ἐρωτήματα (Milan, 1476. First Greek book ever printed).

Cf. Voigt, I 371, II 148; A. F. Villemain, Lascaris, Paris, 1825 (Engl. transl. 1875, London).

(B). Italian Humanists.

   (1). *Francesco Petrarca*, 1304–74.

Discoverer of Cicero's Letters.

Cf. Voigt, I, pp. 12–159; Symonds, pp. 69–87; Th. Campbell, Life and Times of Petrarca, 1845²; G. Körting, P. Leben u. Werke, Lpz. 1878.

   (2). *Giovanni Boccaccio*, 1313–75.

   a. Genealogia deorum gentilium.

   b. De casibus illustrium virorum.

c. De claris mulieribus.

d. De montibus, silvis, fontibus, lacubus, fluminibus.

Cf. *G. Koerting*, B.'s Leben u. Werke, pp. 742, Lpz. 1880; Voigt, I, pp. 165-86; Symonds, pp. 87-97, 133.

(3). *Colutius Salutatus* (Coluccio de Piero de Salutati), 1330–1406.

Cf. Voigt, I 194-214, II 192, 486; Symonds, p. 103 ff.

(4). *Leonardo Bruni* (Aretinus), 1369-1444.

Celebrated translations of *Aristotle*, Demosthenes, Plutarch.

Cf. Voigt, I 309 ff., II 165 ff.

(5). *Francesco Poggio Bracciolini*, 1380-1459.

Discoverer of MSS of *Cicero* (seven orations), Asconius Pedianus' Commentary to Cicero's speeches, *Plautus* (XII new comedies), a complete *Quintilian*, Ammianus Marcellinus, Aratea, Silius, Manilius, Columella, Frontinus, *Nonius*, Probus, *Petronius*, parts of *Lucretius*, Valerius Flaccus, Priscian, Vitruvius, Statius' Silvae [*Tacitus*, Dial., Germ., *Suet.* de gramm.].

Cf. Voigt, I 237-62, II 7, 75, 254 ff., 329 ff.; Symonds, p. 134 ff., 230-46; Henzen in C. I. L. VI 1 (on P.'s contributions to epigraphy).

(6). *Victorinus da Feltre*, 1379-1447.

Celebrated pedagogue.

Cf. Voigt, I 537 ff.; Symonds, pp. 289-97.

(7). *Kyriacus of Ancona*, 1391-c. 1450.

"I go to awake the dead." Famous collector of inscriptions in Greece and Italy.

Cf. *Voigt*, I 271-88; C. I. L. III, p. xxii, 129 ff.; *E. Hübner*, Röm. Epigraphik (= I. Müller's Handbuch, vol. I, p. 475 ff.); Symonds, p. 155 ff.

(8). *Giovanni Aurispa*, c. 1370-1459.

Famous collector of Greek MSS. Reached *Venice* in 1423, with 238 *vols.*, containing mostly classical authors purchased in Constantinople. Among his priceless treasures were the celebrated codex Laurentianus (seven plays of *Soph.*, six of *Aesch.; Apollonius*, Argonautica), of the X. cent., now in Florence; the entire *Demosthenes*, and *Plato, Xenophon, Diodorus, Strabo, Arrian, Lucian, Dio Cassius*.

Cf. Voigt, I 262 ff., 560 ff., II 348.

(9). *Francesco Filelfo* (Philelphus), 1398–1481.
Itinerant professor; collector of MSS. Translator of Homer.
Cf. Voigt, I 351–69; Symonds, pp. 267–89.

(10). *Laurentius Valla* (Lorenzo della Valle), 1407–57.
a. *Elegantiae Latini sermonis*, 1444. 59. edit. in 1536. Still useful.
b. Translations: Herodotus, Thucydides, Homer.
c. Edition of *Quintilian*, printed 1494.
Cf. *I. Vahlen*, Lorenzo Valla, Vienna, 1870; Voigt, I 464–80, II 181 f.; Symonds, pp. 258–65.

(11). *Marsilius Ficinus* (Marsiglio Ficino), 1433–99.
Famous translation of *Plato*.
Cf. Creuzer, Opusc. II 5, pp. 10–21; Voigt, II 123, 326; Symonds, p. 324 ff.

(12). *Angelus Politianus* (Angiolo de' Ambrosini of Monte Puliciano), 1454–98.
Praefationes to Homer, Quintilian, Statius' Silvae, Suetonius, Praelectio in Persium. Translation of *Callimachus*, Herodianos and Epictetus.
Cf. *Heeren*, l. c., II 247–69; Voigt, I 371, II 199; Symonds, pp. 345–55.

(13). *Petrus Victorius* (Pietro Vettori), 1499–1584.
The greatest philologist and critic of the Italian Renaissance.
a. Edition of Cicero, with commentary.
b. Edition of *Sophocles*, with comment. and the scholia, 1547. The *Electra* published for the first time in 1545. *Aeschylus*, 1557.
c. Edition, commentary and translation of *Aristotle* (Ethics, Rhetoric, Poetics, de partibus animalium, Politics).
d. Xenophon's Memorabilia.
e. Terence; Sallust; Varro, de re rustica.
f. Demetrius [Phalereus] de elocutione, Dionysius, Isaeus, Dinarchus, Hipparchus in Arati et Eudoxi Phaenomena, Clemens Alexandrinus, Porphyrius de abstinentia.
g. *Variae lectiones*, 38 bks.
Cf. *Bandini*, Petri Victorii vita, Florence, 1758; *Fr. Creuzer*, l. c., pp. 21–36; *H. Kämmel*, Jahn's Jahrb. 95, p. 545 ff.; 96, p. 325 ff., 421 ff.

A List of the More Important Editiones Principes of
Classical Authors.

Cf. Chr. Saxe, Onomasticon, 2 vols., 1775–90; *I. I. Brunet*, Manuel de
Libraire, etc., 8 vols., 1880; *F. A. Schweiger*, Handbuch d. class. Bibliographie, 2 vols., 1830–34; *S. F. G. Hoffmann*, Lex. Bibliographicum, 3
vols. (only Greek authors), 1832; *L. Hain*, Repertorium bibliographicum,
ab arte typographia inventa usque ad a. MD, 4 vols., Paris and Stuttgart,
1838.

1. *Greek.*
1481. Theocritos (Id. I–XVIII), together with Hesiod, Works
and Days.
1488. Homer (ed. Chalcondylas). Valla's Latin transl. of the
Iliad printed as early as 1474.
1495. Hesiod, Opera omnia (Aldus).
1495–98. Aristotle (Aldus).
1496. Euripides' Med., Hypp., Alc., Androm. (I. Lascaris),
Apollonius (Lascaris), Lucian (in Florence).
1498. Aristophanes (excl. Lys. and Thesm.); Opera omnia.
Basle, 1532.
1499. Aratus (in: Astronomi vett. ap. Aldum).
1500. Callimachus' Hymns (Lascaris).
1502. Herodotus, Thucydides, Sophocles (Aldi).
1503. Euripides' Opera (excl. Electra, edit. by Victorius, 1545,
from Cod. Laurent. 32, 2).
1513. Plato, Oratt. Att. [Hyperides, papyrus discovered 1847].
Pindar (together with Callim., Dionys., Perierg., Lycophron) (Aldus).
1514. Athenaeus (Aldus).
1516. Xenophon (excl. Agesil., Apologia, Πόροι, ap. Iunta),
Opera omnia, 1525, ap. Aldum; Strabo (transl. printed
in Rome, 1470), Pausanias.
1518. Aeschylus (Aldus).
1530. Polybius (ap. Vincent. Opsopocus, *i. e.* Koch). Latin
transl. by Nic. Perrotto (bks. I–V), printed 1473.
1533. Diogenes Laertius (Froben, Basle).
1539. Diodorus (libb. 16–20). Latin transl. (libb. I–V) by
Poggio, 1472.
1544. Iosephus (Basle).
1548. Cassius Dio (R. Stephanus).
1551. Appian.
1572. Plutarch (H. Stephanus). Latin transl. by Campanus,
1471.

2. *Latin.*

1465. Cicero, de officiis. First printed edition of a classical author. Cf. art. 'Typography' in Encycl. Brit. Lactantius (Rome).

1469. Caesar, Virgil, Livy, Lucan, Apuleius, Gellius (Rome).

1470. Persius, Iuvenal, Martial, Quintilian, Suetonius (Rome). Tacitus, Iuvenal, Sallust, Horace (Venice). Terence (Strassburg).

1471. Ovid (Rome, Bonn), Nepos (Venice).

1472. Plautus (G. Merula), Catullus, Tibullus, Propertius, Statius (Venice).

1473. Lucretius (Brixiae).

1474. Valerius Flaccus (Bonn).

1475. Seneca (Prose Works), Sallust (*first* volume issued in *octavo*).

1484. Seneca (Tragedies) at Ferrara.

1485. Pliny the Younger (Venice).

1498. Cicero, Opera omnia.

1520. Vell. Paterculus (Beatus Rhenanus, Basle). Only one MS in existence.

V. FRANCE.

Cf. *E. Egger*, L'Hellénisme en France, 2 vols. 1869.

(1) *Robert Etienne* (Stephanus), 1503–69.
    Learned printer of classical authors, e. g. Horace, Dionysius Halic. Dio Cassius. *Thesaurus* linguae Latinae, 1531–6.

(2) HENRI ETIENNE, son of Robert, 1528–98.
    For a list of the extremely numerous editions of this famous printer cf. L. Feugère, Essai sur la vie et les ouvrages de H. E., Paris, 1853. Cp. also Pökel, l. c. sub nomine.
    Thesaurus graecae linguae, 5 vols., 1572; re-edited by Dindorf, 1865. Still the most complete lexicon of Greek published.
    Cf. *Egger*, l. c. p. 198 ff.

(3) *Adrien Turnebous* (Turnebus), 1512–65.
    Celebrated *critic*. Editor e. g. Aesch. *Soph.*, Arist. Ethics, Theophrastus, Philo., *Cicero, de legg.* Commentaries to *Varro*, de ling. Lat., and Horace, *Adversaria*, 30 bks. Cf. Pökel s. v.

(4) Denis Lambin (Dionysius Lambinus), 1520–72.
    Famous commentator and critic of *Horace, Cicero, Lu-
    cretius, Plautus*, Nepos.
    Cf. Orelli, Onomasticon Ciceronis, vol. I, Appendix, pp. 478–91.
(5) Marcus Antonius Muretus, 1526–85.
    Renowned Latin stylist and critic.
    Editions and commentaries to *Terence, Catullus, Tibul-
    lus, Propertius*, Seneca; *Cicero, Philippics. Variae
    lectiones.*
    Cf. Opera omnia, ed. *D. Ruhnken*, 4 vols. 1789 (Life in vol. IV, pp. 518–
    82), and *C. Dejob*, M. A. Muret, Paris, 1881 (IV pp. 496).
    On *Scaliger*, see below.
(6) Isaac Casaubon (Casaubonus), 1559–1614.
    Next to Scaliger the greatest πολυίστωρ of his time.
    a. *De Satyrica Graeca poesi et Romanorum satira*, 1605
       (ed. Rambach, Halle, 1774).
    b. Editions and commentaries:
       a. *Theophrastus*, Characters. 1592.
       β. *Athenaeus*, 1598. 1840⁸ (incorporated into Schweig-
          häuser's edition).
       γ. *Persius*, 1605. 1833⁴.
       δ. *Suetonius*, 1595. 1611³ (cf. F. A. Wolff's edition).
       ε. *Polybius*, 1609. (Especially noteworthy for its introduc-
          tion on *Greek historiography*.)
       ζ. Apuleius, Strabon, Polyaenos (ed. pr.) Histor. Aug.
          Script., Aristophanes.
       η. Exegetical and critical contributions to Dionysius Halic.,
          Pliny the Younger, Theocritos, Diogenes Laertius.
    Cf. *Mark Pattison*, Isaac Casaubon, Oxford, 1892² (ed. Nettleship).
    On *Salmasius*, see below.
(7) Charles du Fresne sieur *du Cange*, 1610–88.
    a. *Glossarium ad scriptores mediae et infimae Latinitatis*,
       1678.
    b. Glossarium ad scriptores mediae et infimae Graecitatis,
       1688.
    c. Edition of Byzantian Historians, 1680.
    Cf. *Hardouin*, Essai sur la vie et les ouvrages de du Cange, Paris, 1849.
(8) *Bernhard de Montfaucon*, 1655–1741.
    Cf. *E. de Broglie*, La société de l'abbaye de Saint-Germain, etc., 1891,
    2 vols.

a. Palaeographia Graeca, 1708 f.

b. L'antiquité expliquée et représentée en figures, 10 vols. fol. (1719), Suppl. 5 vols. fol. (1724). 1757².

VI. THE NETHERLANDS.

Cf. *L. Müller*, Gesch. der class. Philologie in den Niederlanden, Lpz. 1869 (pp. 249).

Desiderius Erasmus of Rotterdam, 1465–1536.

Cf. *R. B. Drummond*, E., his Life and Character, 2 vols., London, 1873 ; L. Feugère, Erasme, Paris, 1874; A. R. Pennington, Life and Character of E., London, 1875 ; Pökel, l. c. p. 71 f.; *Adagiorum Chiliades* (1506).

1. FIRST PERIOD, 1530–75.
   (1) Adriaan de Jonghe (*Hadrianus Junius*), 1511–75.
      Plutarch, Symp., Martial, Nonius Marcellus, Animadversiones, 6 bks.—nomenclator octilinguis.
   (2) *Jacob de Crusque* (Cruquius), †1584.
      Editor of *Horace* with scholia, 1578.
   (3) *Wilhelm Canter*, 1541–75.
      Editions of Aesch., Soph., Eur., Aristides, Stobaeus. Transl. of Lycophron's Alexander (in Scaliger's edition).

2. SECOND PERIOD, 1575–1650.
   Foundation of the University of Leiden, 1575: Utrecht, 1636. Cf. L. Müller, p. 5 ff. Characteristic of the period.
   (1) JUSTUS LIPSIUS, 1547–1606.
      1567 in Rome, 1572 Professor in Jena, 1576 in Löwen, *1579* in Leiden, 1592 in Löwen.
      a. TACITUS, 1574¹. Epoch-making masterpiece.
      b. *Velleius Paterculus*, 1591. Cf. Ruhnken, Opusc. II, p. 541.
      c. *Seneca* Philosophus, 1605.
      d. Valerius Maximus.

   Cf. A. de Reiffenberg, De J. L. vita et scriptis commentarius, Brussels, 1823; L. Müller, pp. 24–29, 33–35.

   (2) JOSEPH JUSTUS SCALIGER, 1540–1609.
      One of the greatest scholars of all times. *Wyttenbach*, Praef. ad Plut. Moralia ' Unus forte Joseph Scaliger, quem ex omnibus qui post renatas Literas fuerunt, omni Antiquitatis scientia consumatissimum fuisse constat, non multum ab hac perfectione abfuit.' Born in France. Called to Leiden in 1593.

a. Coniectanea to Varro, De L. L., 1565.

b. Catalecta Virgilii et aliorum poetarum veterum, 1572.

c. FESTUS, 1575.

d. *Catullus, Tibullus, Propertius,* 1577.

e. Manilius, 1579.

f. DE EMENDATIONE TEMPORUM, 1583.

g. THESAURUS TEMPORUM, 1606.

h. TWENTY-FOUR INDEXES TO GRUTER'S THESAURUS INSCRIPT. LATIN., 1601.

i. De re nummaria, 1616 ; Opuscula, 1610 ; De arte critica, 1619.

Cf. *J. Bernays,* J. J. Scaliger, Berlin, 1855 (pp. 319) ; List of works, l. c. p. 267–305 ; *L. Müller,* pp. 35, 222–7 ; *M. Pattison,* The Lives of the two Scaligers, London, 1856 ; *Ruhnkenius,* Elog. Hemsterhusii (Opusc. I 269).

(3) *Gerhard Johannes Vossius,* 1577–1649.
1615 in Leiden, 1622 in Amsterdam.

a. Grammatica Latina (1607), *Aristarchus* (1635), de vitiis sermonis (1640), Etymologicum (1660).

b. Ars rhetorum, de arte poetica (1647).

c. DE HISTORICIS GRAECIS, 1634 (1833 ed. Westermann).

d. De historicis Latinis, 1627.

Cf. L. Müller, p. 39 f. ; Pökel, s. v.

(4) *Daniel Heinsius,* 1581–1639.
Editor of Hesiod, Theocritos, Terence, Virgil, Horace, *Ovid,* Seneca, *Silius.* Cf. L. Müller, p. 38 f.

(5) Claude de Saumaise (*Salmasius*), 1588–1653.
Professor in Leiden, 1631. At the court of Christina of Sweden, 1650. Opponent of Milton. Discoverer of Kephalas' Anthologia, 1606.
" Non homini sed scientiae deest quod nescivit Salmasius."—Balzac.

a. Hist. Aug. Scriptt. 1620 ; Florus, 1609 ; Tertullian.

b. *Plinianae exercitatt.* in Solinum, 1629.

c. De lingua hellenistica, 1643.

d. De usuris, de mutuo, de annis climactericis.

e De re militari Romanorum, 1657.

Cf. Saxe, Onomast. IV 188 ff. ; F. Creuzer, l. c. pp. 65–75 ; L. Müller, p. 41.

(6) *Hugo Grotius,* 1583–1645.

a. Famous transl. of the *Anthol. Planudea,* 1645.

b. De iure belli et pacis, 1625[1].

c. Editions of: Mart. Capella, Lucan's Pharsalia, Silius Italicus.

Cf. Creuzer, l. c. p. 80 ff.; L. Müller, p. 38 ; Pökel. s. v.

3. THIRD PERIOD, 1650–1750.

  (1) Joh. Friedrich *Gronov*, 1611–1671.
    Editor of: Sallust, Seneca the elder, Plinius, Tacitus, Gellius, Justinus, Plautus, Phaedrus, Statius, Martial. Cf. L. Müller, pp. 42–44.

  (2) Jacob *Gronov*, 1645–1716, son of (1).
    a. Editor of: Herodotus, Polybius, Cicero, Ammianus.
    b. Thesaurus Antiquitatum Graecarum, 13 vols., 1702.

  (3) *Nicolaus Heinsius* (son of Daniel H.), 1620–81.
    Editions and commentaries of: Virgil, Ovid, Valerius Flaccus, Silius, Claudianus, Prudentius, Petronius, Velleius, Curtius, Tacitus. Cf. L. Müller, pp. 51–54.

  (4) Joh. Georg *Graevius*, 1623–1703.
    Editor of: *Cicero*, Opera omnia, Hesiod, Callimachus, Justinus, Catullus, Tibullus, Propertius, Florus. *Thesaurus antiquitatum Romanorum*, 12 vols., 1699. Cf. L. Müller, p. 44 f.

  (5) *Ezechiel Spanheim*, 1629–1710.
    Born in Geneva, died in London. Educated in Leiden.
    a. Famous and still useful commentary to the *Hymns* of *Callimachus*, ed. Ernesti, 1761, in 2 vols.
    b. Dissertatio *de usu et praestantia numismatum antiquorum*, 1664, 1706[2].

    Cf. D. Ruhnken, Opusc. II 596 f.

  (6) *Peter Burmann* the elder, 1668–1741.
    Editor of: Petronius, Velleius, Quintilian, Suetonius, Aristophanes, Phaedrus, Lucan, Valerius Flaccus.

    Cf. L. Müller, pp. 45, f. 54–59; Saxe, Onomast. V pp. 466–77.

  (7) Peter *Burmann* [Secundus], nephew of (6), 1714–78.
    Editor of: Virgil, Propertius, Claudianus, *Poetae Minores, Anthologia Latina*.

    Cf. *T. C. Harles*, Vitae Philologorum nostra aetate clarissimorum, vol. I, pp. 93–167.

  (8) Tiberius Hemsterhuis (HEMSTERHUSIUS), 1685–1766.
    Prof. in Franeker 1717, in Leiden 1740.

Edition of *Pollux, Lucian* and *Aristoph. Plutos.*

Cf. D. Ruhnken, Elogium H. (= Opusc. I 238 ff.) ; L. Müller, pp. 74-82.

4. FOURTH PERIOD, 1750 to the present.
  (1) Ludwig Caspar *Valckenaer*, 1750-85.
      Prof. in Franeker, 1741 ; in Leiden, 1766.
      a. Editions of: Homer, Iliad with scholia, 1747.
      EURIPIDIS PHOENISSAE, 1755 (1824⁴, Lpz. 2 vols.).
      Euripidis Hippol. acced. DIATRIBE IN EUR. PERDIT.
      FABB. RELL. 1768 (1823, Lpz. 2 vols.).
      THEOCRITOS, *Bion and Moschus*, 1781. Poetae bucolici
      et didactici ed. ill. 1781.
      Callimachi fragmenta, ed. Luzac, 1799.
      b. DIATRIBE DE ARISTOBULO ed. Luzac, 1806.
      F. Ursinus, *Vergilius* collatione scriptt. Graec. illustr. ed.
      Valck, 1747.

      Cf. Wyttenbach, Opusc. I 796; L. Müller, p. 82 f.

  (2) David Ruhneken (RHUNKENIUS), 1723-98.
      Prof. at Leiden.
      a. *Timaei lexicon* vocum Platonicarum, 1754 (1833⁴).
      b. Oratio de doctore umbratico, Leiden, 1761.
      c. *Historia critica oratorum Graecorum*, 1768 (Lpz. 1841).
      d. (P. J. Schardam) De vita et scriptis *Longini.*
      e. Velleius, Homeric Hymns to Demeter and Dionysos.
      f. Dictata in Terentium, in Ovidii Heroidas, in Suetonium.

      Cf. *D. Wyttenbach,* Vita D. Ruhnkenii, ed. Bergmann, 1824; L. Müller,
      pp. 84-8, 101-3.

  (3) *Daniel Wyttenbach*, 1746-1820.
      a. PLUTARCHI MORALIA (Text, Animadversiones, index,
      14 vols.; Commentary unfinished), 1795-1820. Plato's
      Phaedo.
      b. Philomathia, 3 vols., 1817. Bibliotheca Critica, 1779-
      1809. Vita Ruhnkenii, 1790, pp. 295.

      Cf. L. Müller, pp. 91-6.

  (4) *Peter Hofmann-Peerlkamp*, 1786-1865.
      Editions of: Tacitus' Agricola, *Horace*, Odes (1834),
      Satires (1845) and Ars Poetica (1863), Virgil, Aeneid
      (1863). Propertius, 1865. Cf. L. Müller, p. 110 f.

  (5) *C. Gabriel Cobet*, 1813-88.
      Prof. in Leiden.

a. Oratio de arte interpretandi, 1847.
b. Diogenes Laertius, Paris, 1850.
c. Novae Lectiones, 2 vols. Variae Lectiones, 2 vols.
Cf. J. J. Hartmann, Biogr. Jahrbuch (Calvary), XII p. 53 ff. (1889).

VII. ENGLAND.

Burney's Pleiad: Bentley, [Dawes,] Markland, Taylor, [Toup, Tyrwhitt,] Porson.

(1) RICHARD BENTLEY, 1662–1742.
   1676 in Cambridge, 1689 in Oxford, 1694 in London, 1700 Master of Trinity College, Cambridge.
   a. Epistola ad Millium, 1691.
   b. DISSERTATION ON THE EPISTLES OF PHALARIS, etc., 1690 (ed. W. Wagner, 1874). Immortal masterpiece.
   c. HORACE, 1711. 1869 (ed. Zangemeister). 'Epoch-making masterpiece.'
   d. Discovery of the *Digamma* in *Homer* (Collins on Free-thinking, 1713, ed. of Milton, 1732).
   e. Terence (Famous introduction on *Latin versification*), · with Phaedrus, Publilius Syrus, 1726.
   f. Collection of the fragments of CALLIMACHUS, 1693.
   g. Manilius (1739); Emendations to Menander and Philemon (1710).
   Cf. *J. H. Monk*, Life of R. B., 2 vols. 1833² (I pp. 428, II 466); *F. A. Wolff*, Literar. Analecten I 1–95, II 493–9 (= Klein. Schrift. II 1030, 1089 ff.); *R. C. Jebb*, R. B. (Engl. Men of Letters), Lond. 1882 (pp. 224): *O. Mähly*, R. B., 1868 (pp. 179). Bernays, Philol. Mus. VIII 1–24.

(2) *Jeremiah Markland*, 1693–1776.
   Editor of *Euripides*, Maximus Tyrius, *Statius Silvae*. Remarks on the *Epistles of Cicero to Brutus*, 1745.
   Cf. Wolff, Analecten, II 370–91.

(3) *John Taylor*, 1703–66.
   Editor of *Lysias*, 1739; Aeschines, 1769; several orations of Demosthenes.
   Cf. Wolff, l. c. I 500 ff.

(4) RICHARD PORSON, 1759–1808.
   Next to Bentley, England's greatest text critic. Prof. in Cambridge, 1792; Librarian of the London Institution, 1805.
   a. Aeschylus, 1795, 2 vols.

b. EURIP. HECUBA, 1797, with suppl. to the famous preface
on *Greek versification* [Canon Porsonianum], 1808.
c. Eurip. Orest. 1798 ; Phoen. 1799 ; Medea, 1801.
d. Critical contributions to Homer, Herodotus, Xenophon,
Aristoph., Pausanias, Suidas (cf. Tracts and Miscella-
neous Criticism of R. P., ed. by Kidd, 1815).
Cf. *J. S. Watson,* Life of R. P., 1861 ; F. A. Wolff, Anal. II 284–9 ;
G. Hermann, Opusc. VI 92 ff.

(5) *Peter Elmsley,* 1713–1825.
Editions of: Thucydides, *Eurip.,* Alc., Androm., Elect.,
Med., Heracl., Bacch., *Aristoph.,* Acharn., with comment., 1809. Soph., O. T., O. C.
(6) William Martin *Leake,* 1777–1869.
Celebrated traveler and archaeologist.
a. Topography of Athens and the demi.
b. Travels in Northern Greece, 1841, 4 vols.
c. Travels in the Morea, 1830, 2 vols.
Cf. *E. Curtius,* Alterthum u. Gegenwart, p. 305 ff.

(7) *Thomas Gaisford,* 1779–1855.
Edition of: *Hephaestion, Procli* Chrestom., *Suidas,* 3
vols., Scriptt. lat. rei metricae, Paroemiogr. Graec.,
Etymol. Magn., Stobaeus, Eusebius, 6 vols.
(8) *George Grote,* 1794–1871.
a. GREEK HISTORY, 12 vols., 1856.
b. Plato and the other companions of Socrates, 1865.
c. Aristotle (unfinished), 1871.
(9) Hugh Andrew Johnstone *Munro,* 1819–85.
a. LUCRETIUS (text, comment., transl.), 3 vols., 1873.
1886'.
b. Lucil. Aetna, text and comment., 1867.
c. Horace, 1869.
d. Criticisms and Elucidations of *Catullus,* 1878.
Cf. J. D. Duff, Biogr. Jahrb. VII p. 111 ff.

VIII. GERMANY.
Chief work: *C. Bursian,* Geschichte der class. Philologie von den
Anfängen bis zur Gegenwart, Munich, 1883 (VIII pp. 1271); Hübner,
l. c. pp. 99–121.

(*A*) ANTE-WOLFFIAN PERIOD.
(1) Roclef Huysman (*Rudolphus Agricola*), 1442/3–85.

Famous pedagogue. The first to introduce the system-
atic study of the classics into Germany. Translation
of Ps. Plato, Axiochus, several treatises of Lucian,
Commentary to Seneca Rhetor.

Cf. Bursian, p. 101 f.

(2) *Johannes* REUCHLIN, 1455–1522.
   a. Vocabularius brevíloquus, synopsis grammaticae
   Graecae.
   b. Translation of the Batrachomyomachia.
   c. Editions of: *Xenophon*, Apol. Agesil. Hiero; Aeschinis
   et Demosthenis oratt. adversariae.

Cf. L. Geiger, R., sein Leben u. seine Werke, Berl. 1871; Bursian, pp.
120–31.

(3) Joachim Kammermeister (*Camerarius*), 1500–74.
   a. Editions of: Speeches of Demosth., Sophocles, with
   commentary (1534, 1556), Quintilian, with comment.
   (1534), Cicero, 4 vols. fol., 1540, Herodotus, Thucydides,
   Plautus (1552), Theocritos, Aristotle's Ethics, Theo-
   phrastos, historia rei nummariae.

Cf. Ritschl, Opusc. II 99 ff., III 67 ff. (On his edition of Plautus);
Bursian, pp. 185–90. Full list of works in Pökel, s. v. p. 39 f.

(4) Johann Albert *Fabricius*, 1668–1736.
   a. Bibliotheca Graeca, 14 vols., 1728 (ed. Harles, 1809, 12
   vols., index, 1838). A monumental and still indispensable
   storehouse of information.
   b. Bibliotheca Latina, 1697 (ed. Ernesti, 1773).
   c. Bibliotheca Lat. med. et infim. aetatis, 1746, 6 vols.
   d. Sextus Empiricus, 1718.

Cf. H. S. Reimarus, de vita et scriptis F. Hamburg, 1737; Creuzer, pp.
201–5; Bursian, pp. 360–4; Pökel, s. v.

(5) Johann Matthias *Gesner*, 1691–1761.
   Editions of: *Scriptores rei rusticae*, Horace, Quintilian,
   Pliny the Younger, Claudianus. *Thesaurus Linguae
   Latinae*, 2 vols. fol., 1749. Transl. of *Lucian.*

Cf. Bursian, pp. 387–93; F. Paulsen, Gesch. d. gelehrt. Unterrichts in
Deutschl., Lpz. 1885, pp. 427–40.

(6) Johann August *Ernesti*, 1707–81.
   Editions of: Xenophon, Memorab., Arist. Clouds, Homer, Callimachus Polybius, Tacitus, Sueton., *Cicero,*

1739, 1774, 5 vols., with clavis Ciceroniana (Halle, 1832²). Famous teacher and Latin stylist.

Cf. Bursian, pp. 400–4; Allg. deutsche Biogr. VI 235–42.

(7) Joh. Jacob REISKE, 1716–74.
> *a.* Edition of Constantinos Porphyrogennetos, de cerimoniis aulae Byzantinae, 2 vols., 1754.
> *b.* Editions of: Theocritos, 2 vols., 1766 ; *Oratt. Graeci*, 12 vols., 1775.
> (*c*) Editions of: *Plutarch*, 12 vols.; *Dionysius Halic.*, 6 vols.; *Maximos Tyrios*, 2 vols.; Dion. Chrysostomos, 2 vols.; Libanios, 4 vols. (all printed after R.'s death).
> *d.* Translation of: Speeches in Thucyd., Speeches of *Dem. and Aesch*, 5 vols.
> *e. Animadversiones ad auctores Graecos*, 5 vols., 1766.

Cf. Autobiography, Lpz. 1783 ; Bursian, pp. 407–16.

(8) Johann Joachim WINCKELMANN, 1717–68.
> Founder of the science of Archaeology.
> *Die Geschichte der Kunst des Alterthums*, 1764.

Cf. *K. Justi*, W., sein Leben, seine Werke und seine Zeitgenossen, 3 vols., Lpz., 1872 (pp. xii + 525, 398, pp. vi + 440); Bursian, pp. 426–36.

(9) Joseph Hilarius ECKHEL, 1737–98.
> Founder of the science of Numismatics.
> *Doctrina nummorum veterum*, 8 vols., 1798. 1841'.

Cf. Bursian, pp. 496–99.

(10) Christian Gottlob HEYNE, 1729–1812.
> Editions of: Tibullus, 1755; Epictetus, 1756 ; *Virgil*, 4 vols., 1775; Pindar, [Ps.] *Apollodori Bibliotheca*, 2 vols., 1782, 1802²; *Iliad*, 8 vols., 1802; *Opusc. Academica*, 6 vols., 1785–1812.

Cf. *A. H. L. Heeren*, Chr. G. Heyne, Göttingen, 1813 (XXII, pp. 522) ; Bursian, pp. 476–500.

(*B*) THE NEW SCHOOL.
> Friedrich August WOLFF, 1759 (200 years after Casaubonus) –1824.
> *a.* Prolegomena to HOMER, 1795. Cp. R. Volckmann, Geschichte u. Kritik der W.'s Prolegg., Lpz. 1874.
> *b.* Demosthenis Leptinea (valuable introduction), 1790.

46

c. Plato's Symposium, Hesiod, Theogony; Cicero, Tusc. Disp., *Orations* (Post red. in senatu, ad Quirites, de domo sua, de haruspicum responsis, pro Marcello— regarded as spurious by W.), Aristoph. *Clouds*, Casaubonus' Suetonius.

d. Encyclopaedie der Philologie ed. Stockmann, Lpz. 1831.

e. Kleine Schriften, 2 vols. (pp. 1200), Ed. G. Bernhardy, 1869.

Cf. W. Körte, Leben u. Studien F. A. W.'s des Philologen, 2 vols., Essen, 1833 (pp. 363, 314); Bursian, pp. 517-48.

1. *Grammatico-critical School.*
On *Criticism* and *Hermeneutics:*

F. *Schleiermacher,* Works, III 3, p. 344 ff.; Hermeneutik u. Kritik, Works, 1 pt. VII, 1838 (pp. xviii + 390); G. *Hermann,* de officio interpretis, Opusc. V, p. 405 ff., VII 97 ff.; A. *Boeckh,* Opusc. I 100 ff., V 248 ff., VII 262 ff., Encyclopaedie, etc., der phil. Wissensch., pp. 79-263; H. *Sauppe,* Epistola Critica; C. G. *Cobet,* Oratio de arte interpretandi, Leiden, 1847 (pp. 163); J. N. *Madvig,* Advers. Critica, I (1871) pp. 8-184; E. *Tournier,* Exercises critiques, Paris, 1875 (pp. 175); Fr. *Blass,* Hermeneutik u. Kritik (Iwan Müller's Handbuch) I (1886), pp. 125-272.

(1) Gottfried HERMANN, 1772-1848.
   a. Editions of: *Aeschylus,* Soph., *Eurip.* (Hecuba, Herc. fur. Suppl. *Bacchae,* Alcestis, *Ion*), Arist. Clouds, *Plautus'* Trinummus, *Aristotle's Poetics, Homeric Hymns,* Lexicon of Photios, Bion and Moschus.
   b. *Elementa doctrinae metricae,* 1816.
   c. *Homeric* treatises, 1832, 1840. *Opusc.,* 8 vols., 1827-39. vol. VIII, 1876.

Cf. O. Jahn, Biogr. Aufsätze, Lpz. 1849 (pp. 91-132); Bursian, p. 575 ff., pp. 666-86.

(2) Christian August *Lobeck,* 1781-1860.
   a. *Sophocles, Aiax,* 1809.
   b. *Aglaophamus,* 2 vols., 1829.
   c. Paralipomena grammaticae Graecae, 2 vols., 1837.

Cf. Bursian, p. 572 ff., 711-713.

(3) August Immanuel BEKKER, 1785-1881.
   a. Text Editions of: Plato, Attic Orators, Aristotle, Sextus Empiricus, Thucydides, Theognis, Aristophanes, Photios, Suidas, Scholia to the Iliad, Cassius Dio, Harpocration,

Corpus scriptt. Byzantinorum, 24 vols., Homer (with *digamma* in the text), etc., etc.

Cf. Bursian, pp. 658–63; Pökel, s. v.

(4) *Karl Lachmann*, 1793–1831.

a. Propertius (1816), *Catullus, Prop.*, *Tibull.*, 1829, Terentianus Maurus.

b. BETRACHTUNGEN ÜBER HOMER'S ILIAS (mit Zusätzen von M. Haupt), 1837, 1841. ' Epoch-making.'

c. LUCRETIUS, with critical commentary. ' Immortal masterpiece.'

d. *Lucilius* (ed. Vahlen), Babrios.

Cf. M. Hertz, K. L., Berlin, 1851 (pp. x + 255, xliii); Bursian, pp. 789–800.

(5) *August Meineke*, 1790–1870.

a. Editor of: *Strabo*, Athenaeus, Callimachus, *Aristophanes, Fragmenta Comicorum* (with HISTORY OF GREEK COMEDY), 5 vols., 1841; Theocritos, Horace (application of the four-line strophe).

b. *Analecta Alexandrina*, 1843.

Cf. F. Ranke, A. M., Ein Lebensbild, Lpz. 1871; Bursian, pp. 764–9.

(6) Karl *Wilhelm Dindorf*, 1802–71.

a. Editor of: Aristophanes, *Poetae scenici graeci*, Demosthenes, 9 vols., 1846–51, *Stephanus Byzantius, Aristides*, Themistios, Lucian, Herodotus, Josephus, *Clemens Alexandrinus*, 4 vols., Eusebius, 4 vols.

b. Scholia to Odyssee, 1856; *scholia to Iliad*, 4 vols., 1877.

c. Lexicon Aeschyleum, *Lex. Sophocleum*. New edition of *Stephanus' Greek Thesaurus*, Metra Aesch., Soph., Eur., Aristoph.

Cf. Biogr. Jahrb. VI, 1883, p. 112 ff.; Bursian, pp. 861–70.

(7) *Karl Lehrs*, 1802–78.

a. DE ARISTARCHI STUDIIS HOMERICIS, 1833 (1882², pp. 505).

b. Horace, 1869. Transl. of *Plato's Phaedrus and Symposion*.

c. Die Pindarscholien, Lpz. 1873.

Cf. E. Kammer, Biogr. Jahrb. (1879), pp. 15–28; Bursian, pp. 718–24.

(8) FRIEDRICH RITSCHL, 1806–76.

a. PLAUTUS (*Trinummus*, with famous Prolegg.), Bacchides, PARERGA to Plautus and Terence (*Fabulae Varronianae*, etc.), *Opusc.* vol. II (pp. 782), vol. III, 1–300.

b. On the literary activity of Varro. Opusc. III, pp. 419–592.

c. Aeschylus, Septem, 1853.

d. Priscae latinitatis monumenta epigraphica, 1862. Opusc. vol. V.

e. On Alexandrian library, Stichometry, etc. Opusc. vol. I.

Cf. L. Müller, F. R., Berlin, 1877; *O. Ribbeck,* F. W. R., Ein Beitrag z. Gesch. der Philologie, 2 vols., Lpz. 1881 (pp. vii + 348, viii + 591); Bursian, pp. 812–40.

(9) Johann Nicolaus MADVIG, 1804–86.

a. De Asconii Pediani comment. 1826.

b. CICERO, DE FINIBUS, 1839, 1876².

c. Emendationes *Livianae,* 1860, 1877².

d. Livy, ed. Madvig and Ussing, 1866, 1879³, 4 vols.

e. Latin Grammar, 1843¹. *Greek Syntax,* 1847.

f. Opusc. Acad. 1887². *Adversaria Critica,* 2 vols., 1873.

g. Die Verfassung u. Verwaltung des röm. Staates.

Complete list of his works in Wochenschr. f. class. Philol. IV (1887) p. 285. Cf. Heiberg, Biogr. Jahrb. IX (1886) pp. 202–21.

2. *Historical-antiquarian School.*
   Bibliography :

Greek and Roman Literature, Grammar, Poetics, etc. (Hübner, Encycl. pp. 140–75), Religion (pp. 175–84), Greek and Roman Antiquities and History (pp. 184–215, 359–88), Geography (pp. 215–85), Chronology (pp. 286–90), Archaeology (pp. 290–342), Metrology and Numismatics (pp. 342–51), Epigraphy (pp. 351–59). Cp. also Sal. *Reinach,* Manuel de philologie classique, vol. II, Appendice, Paris, 1884 (pp. 310).

(1) Barthold Georg *Niebuhr,* 1776–1831.

a. ROMAN HISTORY, 3 vols., 1811¹.

b. Lectures on *Roman History,* 3 vols. (Engl. 1843, Germ. 1846).

c. Lectures on *Ancient History,* 3 vols., 1851.

d. Edition of *Fronto,* 1816, Fragmm. of Cicero's Speeches.

e. Kleine Schriften, 2 vols., 1828.

Cf. *S. Winkworth,* The Life and Letters of B. G. N., 3 vols., Lond. 1852 ; Bursian, pp. 647–63 ; F. Eyssenhardt, B. G. N., Gotha, 1886.

(2) August BOECKH, 1785–1867.

a. De Graecae tragoediae principibus, 1806.

b. Edition of PINDAR, 4 vols., 1811–22.

c. CORPUS INSCRIPTIONUM GRAECARUM, 4 vols.

d. PUBLIC ECONOMY OF ATHENS, 12 vols., 1817¹, 1886².

e. Philolaos, 1818.

f. Metrologische Untersuchungen, 1838; Manetho u. die Hundsternperiode, 1845; Zur Gesch. der Mondcyclen, 1856; *Opuscula*, 7 vols., 1874.

g. Encyclopaedie u. Methodologie der Philol. ed. Klussmann, 1886² (pp. 884).

Cf. *E. von Leutsch*, Philol. Anz. XVI (1886) p. 224 ff. ; Bursian, pp. 687–705.

(3) Friedrich Gottlieb *Welcker*, 1784–1868.

a. Die Aeschyleische Trilogie Prometheus, 1824.

b. Theognis, 1826.

c. Der *Epische Cyclus*, 2 vols., 1849 (1882²).

d. DIE GRIECH. TRAGOEDIEN, 3 vols. (pp. 1614), 1841.

e. Alte Denkmäler, 5 vols., 1849–64.

f. Griech. Götterlehre, 3 vols., 1863.

g. Kleine Schriften, 6 vols. (on *Sappho, Prodicus*, etc.).

Cf. Reinh. Kékulé, F. G. W.'s Leben, Lpz. 1880 (pp. 591) ; Bursian, pp. 1029–46.

(4) Karl *Ottfried Müller*, 1797–1840.

a. Die Dorier, 1824; Die Etrusker, 1828 (1878²).

b. Archaeologie der Kunst, 1830 (1878⁴).

c. Aeschylus Eumeniden, 1833.

d. Varro, de lingua Latina, 1833.

e. Festus, 1839.

f. History of the Literature of Ancient Greece, Lond. 1840, 3 vols. (1876² in 3 vols., ed. E. Heitz).

Cf. Bursian, pp. 1007–9 ; *K. Hillebrand*, in the French transl. of (*d*), vol. I, pp. xvii–ccclxxx, Paris, 1865.

(5) Franz BOPP, 1791–1867.

Founder of the science of comparative philology.

Cf. B. Delbrück, Einl. in das Sprachstudium, Lpz. 1880 ; Lefman, F. B., 1892.

(6) *Gottfried Bernhardy*, 1800–75.

a. Eratosthenica, 1822; Dionys. Perieg., 1828 ; Wissensch. Syntax, 1829; SUIDAS, 2 vols., 1834–57.

b. Griech. Literaturgeschichte, 2 vols., 1836–45 (1880).

c. Römische Literaturgesch., 2 vols., 1830 (1872²).

Cf. *R. Volckmann*, G. B., Halle, 1887 (pp. 160); Bursian, p. 776.

(7) *O. Jahn*, 1813–69.

a. Edition and commentary of PERSIUS, 1843 ; *Juvenal,*

1851; Cic. *Orator*, 1851 ; Florus, 1852 ; *Livii Periochae*, 1853; *Soph. Electra*, 1861[1] (1872[2]) ; *Plato, Symposium*, 1864 (1876[3]); *Ps. Longinus* Περὶ ὕψους, 1867 (1887[2]).

b. *Pausaniae descriptio arcis Athen.*, 1860 (1880[2]).

c. Numerous treatises on archaeology and literature (e. g., On the subscriptions in Latin MSS. ' *Ueber den Aberglauben des bösen Blicks* '). Cf. Bursian, pp. 1070–80.

(8) Theodor MOMMSEN, 1817—.

a. *Röm. Münzwesen*, 1850; ROMAN HISTORY, Vols. I–III[2], V[3] (transl. by Dickson); Römische Chronologie, 1859; *Röm. Forschungen*, 2 vols., RÖM. STAATSRECHT, 3 vols. (pp. 708, 1171, 1336), 1888[3].

b. CORPUS INSCRIPTIONUM LATINARUM, Vol. I, III, VIII, IX.

c. *Monumentum Ancyranum*, 1865[1].

d. Zur Lebensgesch. des jüngeren Plinius, Hermes III, pp. 31–139, etc., etc.

For a full list of his works up to 1887 cf. *C. Zangemeister*, Theodor Mommsen als Schriftsteller, Heidelberg, 1887 (pp. 60).

www.ingramcontent.com/pod-product-compliance
Lightning Source LLC
Chambersburg PA
CBHW030721110426
42739CB00030B/1062